By Invitation Only

Artful Entertaining, Southern Style

Junior League of Pensacola, Inc.

*E*ntertaining is an art, but it doesn't have to be complicated. Like the most beautiful paintings and architecture, the best gatherings are usually simple and unpretentious. Pensacola is a place where people often prefer casual, intimate settings with close friends and family. At the same time, however, we enjoy a long and diverse cultural history that provides plenty of occasions for big celebrations!

Pensacola is not an ordinary city and the book you are holding is no ordinary cookbook.
It is arranged as an entertaining guide with chapters centered on popular themes.
Each chapter contains ideas for three different parties and includes recipes, decorating tips
and even sample invitations. An entire chapter is devoted to organizing and planning
in general—a reference guide to be used for every social gathering.

Southerners are known for our hospitality and hosting the perfect party is part of our heritage.
We want to preserve and encourage that tradition. In her famous novel, *Gone With The Wind,*
Margaret Mitchell spoke of Tara as being, "beautiful as a woman who is so sure of her charm that she
can be generous and gracious to all." That is actually the secret to great entertaining—
this book will simply help you with the details.

By Invitation Only

Artful Entertaining, Southern Style
Junior League of Pensacola, Inc.

The Junior League of Pensacola, Inc.
3298 Summit Boulevard, Suite 44
Pensacola, Florida 32503
850-433-4421

© Copyright 2002 by
The Junior League of Pensacola, Inc.
Cover and Chapter Opener art © Copyright Paul Jackson

ISBN: 0-9613622-9-4
Library of Congress Number: 2002101156

Edited, Designed and Manufactured by
Favorite Recipes® Press

FRP™

P.O. Box 305142
Nashville, Tennessee 37230
800-358-0560

Book Design: Brad Whitfield
Production Design: Susan Breining
Art Director: Steve Newman
Project Manager: Ginger Dawson
Project Editor: Jane Hinshaw

Manufactured in the United States of America
First Printing: 2002
15,000 copies

Cookbook Committee

Chairmen: Jennie Baer-Barrow
and Jane Whitehurst
Co-Chairman: Laura Weston
Format Chairman: Shannon Cook
Recipe Chairman: Stacy Brown
Marketing Chairman: Melissa Bailey
Sustaining Advisor: Imogene Kennedy
Non-Recipe Copy Contributor: Dawn Bozeman

Christy Ball
Donna Chilson
Melissa Culbertson
Lucy Donnelly
Connie Gilliam
Lisa Greskovich
Melanie Hamilton
Caroline Hartnett
Blair Hull
Mary Elizabeth Jacobi
Kris Johnson
Julie M. Jones
Julie Barrineau Krehely
Tricia Mangrum
Carolyn McConnell-Reeder
Ginny Ochsner
Tracy Pate
GiGi Peterson
Sam Rodgers
Kristie Rodriguez
Tammy Rogers
Jennipher Scoggins
Brantlee Vinson
Robin Wierzbicki

*P*aul Jackson is considered by many to be the modern master of watercolor. His paintings have garnered critical attention and top awards from the highest ranks of his profession including: the American Watercolor Society, Allied Artists of America, and the Rocky Mountain National Watermedia Society. In 1999, he became the youngest-ever signature member of the American Watercolor Society.

Paul's work hangs in a diversity of collections from the Missouri Governor's Mansion, Supreme Court, and State Capitol to private collections worldwide. Paul received his BFA in Painting from Mississippi State University in 1989, and his MFA in Painting/Illustration from the University of Missouri, Columbia in 1992.

When he is not painting, Paul serves as a judge for major art competitions and is a frequent lecturer at art events worldwide. Paul and his wife, Dina, met at the Greater Gulfcoast Arts Festival in Pensacola in 1992 and were married during the festival in 1994. They opened their first gallery, Illumia, in downtown Columbia, Missouri, in October 2000.

*B*arrett McClean is a resident of Pensacola, Florida. This fun-loving surfer is passionate about every aspect of photography and has actively pursued his dream of being a respected photographer for many years.

Barrett's distinctive style and technical savvy are reflected in every image he captures. From creative family or individual portraits to dramatic black and white documentary-style weddings, Barrett's images are extraordinary.

Barrett's studio is located on the corner of Belmont and Davis in Old East Hill. Married to Beth for three years, they have two children, Thomas and Emory Rose.

*M*ary England Proctor has studied art since her childhood in Birmingham, Alabama. Her first teacher was London Bridges. She earned her BFA Degree in Commercial Design at the University of Alabama with Richard Brough. After moving to Nashville, Tennessee, she had classes with Charles Brindley and Sante Fe artist Stefan Kramer. Mary has exhibited in numerous art shows and has done volunteer art projects for schools and historic sites. Her artwork is in many Southern homes and her miniature "portraits" are in constant demand. Creating custom invitations for forty years, Mary was excited about the challenge of designing the 24 invitations for *By Invitation Only.*

Mary's studio is in Nashville, Tennessee. Married to David for thirty years, they have two married children—David in Nashville, and Josephine Daniels, a member of the Junior League of Pensacola.

Contents

Entertaining by the Numbers

Counting the number of guests is no way to anticipate or measure a party's outcome. Successful gatherings come in a variety of sizes. Choose one of these ideas or adapt one to the number that's right for you. Whether it's small, medium, or large, your party will be an entertaining masterpiece!

TWO IF BY SEA

AFFORDABLE FOR FORTY

FIESTA BRUNCH FOR A BUNCH

Cormorants

Paul Jackson

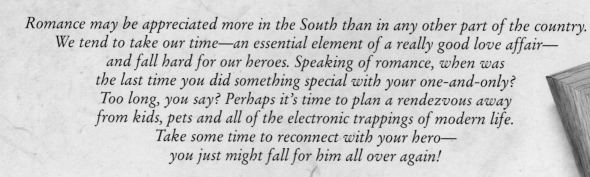

TWO IF BY SEA

*Romance may be appreciated more in the South than in any other part of the country.
We tend to take our time—an essential element of a really good love affair—
and fall hard for our heroes. Speaking of romance, when was
the last time you did something special with your one-and-only?
Too long, you say? Perhaps it's time to plan a rendezvous away
from kids, pets and all of the electronic trappings of modern life.
Take some time to reconnect with your hero—
you just might fall for him all over again!*

BRUSCHETTA

DILLED SHRIMP

GRILLED VEGETABLE PASTA WITH PARSLEY VINAIGRETTE

BERRY-TOPPED CHOCOLATE FUDGE CAKE

WHITE WINE SANGRIA

Bruschetta

1/3 cup (about) olive oil
2 large garlic cloves, chopped
salt and pepper to taste
6 to 8 firm ripe Roma tomatoes, chopped
chopped fresh basil to taste
capers to taste
Tabasco sauce to taste
1 baguette
grated Parmesan cheese to taste

*C*ombine the olive oil, garlic, salt and pepper in a bowl and mix well. Add the tomatoes, basil, capers and Tabasco sauce and stir to coat well.

Cut the baguette into slices and brush with additional olive oil. Place on a baking sheet. Broil until lightly toasted.

For a picnic, place the toasted bread slices in an airtight container. Place the tomato mixture in a separate container. Spoon the tomato mixture onto the bread slices just before serving.

To serve the bruschetta at home, spread the tomato mixture on the bread slices and place on a baking sheet. Sprinkle with grated Parmesan cheese to taste and broil just until the cheese melts. Serve immediately.

Makes 24

Dilled Shrimp

1 tablespoon minced garlic
2 tablespoons minced shallots
2 tablespoons butter or margarine, melted
1 tablespoon olive oil
13/4 pounds large fresh shrimp, peeled and deveined
2 tablespoons lemon juice
4 teaspoons finely chopped fresh dillweed
1/8 teaspoon salt
1/8 teaspoon pepper

*S*auté the garlic and shallots in the butter and olive oil in a large skillet until tender. Stir in the shrimp. Cook over medium heat for 3 minutes or until opaque, stirring occasionally. Add the lemon juice, dillweed, salt and pepper and mix well.

Serve warm or cold. Garnish with lemon slices and additional dillweed if desired.

Serves 8 to 10

WHITE WINE SANGRIA

Combine 4 cups of dry white wine with 1/4 cup orange liqueur and 1/4 cup sugar in a glass pitcher and mix to dissolve the sugar. Add 1 thinly sliced lime, orange and lemon. Cover and chill for 2 hours or longer. Stir in 1 cup chilled club soda just before serving.

Grilled Vegetable Pasta with Parsley Vinaigrette

PARSLEY VINAIGRETTE
1 cup chopped fresh parsley
3 tablespoons red wine vinegar
1 large garlic clove
1/2 cup olive oil
salt and pepper to taste

GRILLED VEGETABLE PASTA
16 ounces fusilli, cooked
2 large ears fresh corn, husked
2 large zucchini, cut into halves lengthwise
1 large red onion, cut into 4 slices
2 tablespoons olive oil
salt and pepper to taste

For the vinaigrette, combine the parsley, vinegar and garlic in a food processor and process until finely chopped. Add the olive oil gradually, processing until smooth. Season with salt and pepper.

For the vegetable pasta, combine the fusilli with enough of the vinaigrette in a bowl to coat well.

Brush the corn, zucchini and onion with the olive oil and arrange on a grill. Grill for 12 minutes or until the vegetables are tender. Cool slightly. Cut the kernels from the corncobs; cut the zucchini and onion into 1/2-inch pieces.

Add the grilled vegetables to the pasta with enough of the remaining vinaigrette to coat well. Season with salt and pepper and toss lightly.

Serves 8

Berry-Topped Chocolate Fudge Cake

3 ounces unsweetened chocolate, chopped
13/4 cups sugar
1/2 cup boiling water
3 eggs
2 tablespoons baking cocoa
9 tablespoons (1 stick plus 1 tablespoon) butter, sliced
3/4 cup sour cream
1 teaspoon vanilla extract
11/4 cups cake flour
11/2 teaspoons baking powder
3/4 teaspoon baking soda
1/2 teaspoon salt
2 cups sweetened whipped cream
1 cup fresh raspberries

Combine the chocolate with 1/2 cup of the sugar in a food processor and process until finely chopped. Add the hot water and process until the chocolate melts. Add the remaining 11/4 cups sugar, eggs and baking cocoa and process for 1 minute. Add the butter and process for 1 minute or until smooth. Add the sour cream and vanilla and process for 5 seconds.

Mix the cake flour, baking powder, baking soda and salt together. Add to the food processor gradually and pulse just until combined; do not overmix.

Spoon into a buttered 9-inch springform pan lined with buttered baking parchment. Bake at 325 degrees on the center oven rack for 1 hour and 20 minutes or until the side of the cake begins to pull away from the side of the pan. Cool in the pan on a wire rack.

For a picnic, take the cake in the springform pan and remove the side at the picnic. Top with the whipped cream and berries to serve.

Serves 12 to 14

Affordable for Forty

When you want to entertain in grand style but have to operate with a less-than-grand budget, pull out the stockpot! Soups are easy to prepare and a cinch to serve. Your guests will feel at home as soon as they step through the door. After all, who can resist the welcoming aroma of homemade soup simmering on the stove? Go ahead! Invite old friends and new—they'll enjoy getting to know each other in a pleasant, casual atmosphere that you've created. Now that's a great party!

Butternut Squash and Apple Soup
Spinach Soup
Wild Rice Soup
Warrington Fish Chowder
Salad Platter
Men's Secret Bleu Cheese Vinaigrette
Cilantro and Lime Vinaigrette
Sun-Dried Tomato Dressing
Olive Bread
Red Pepper Cheese Bread
Cheesy Apple Pie
Chocolate Torte with
Raspberry Sauce

Butternut Squash and Apple Soup

3 butternut squash, peeled and chopped
4 Granny Smith apples, chopped
1/2 medium onion, chopped
8 cups water
3 cups half-and-half or milk
2 garlic cloves, minced
2 tablespoons ground cinnamon
1 tablespoon grated nutmeg
salt and pepper to taste

Combine the squash, apples, onion and water in a large saucepan and simmer until the vegetables and apples are tender. Drain, reserving the cooking liquid.

Process the vegetables and apples in batches in a blender or food processor, adding enough of the reserved cooking liquid to make a smooth consistency. Combine the batches in a saucepan.

Add the half-and-half, garlic, cinnamon, nutmeg, salt and pepper and mix well. Simmer until heated through. Serve hot or cold.

Serves 8

Expect guests to gather in the kitchen at this party, lured by the aromas of the simmering soups. You may even want to serve the soups from the cooking pots. Mix dinnerware patterns, baskets, and pottery for a casual look. Guests will welcome the soup recipes printed on recipe cards to take home as favors.

Spinach Soup

1/4 cup (1/2 stick) butter
1/4 cup all-purpose flour
1 teaspoon celery salt
1/2 teaspoon onion salt
1/2 teaspoon salt
1/4 teaspoon pepper
1/8 teaspoon ground nutmeg
2 cups milk
4 cups hot chicken stock
1 cup cooked fresh spinach, or 1 (10-ounce)
    package frozen chopped spinach, thawed

Melt the butter in a saucepan. Stir in the flour, celery salt, onion salt, salt, pepper and nutmeg. Cook until bubbly, stirring constantly. Add the milk and cook until thickened, stirring constantly.

Add the hot chicken stock and spinach and bring to a boil. Cool slightly.

Process the soup in batches in a blender until smooth. Return to the saucepan and heat to serving temperature. Top servings with whipped cream seasoned with salt if desired.

Serves 10

Wild Rice Soup

1/4 cup (1/2 stick) butter
1 cup chopped onion
1/2 cup chopped celery
1/2 cup chopped carrot
3 cups sliced fresh mushrooms
1/2 cup all-purpose flour
1/2 teaspoon salt
1/2 teaspoon white pepper
4 cups beef broth
2 cups milk or light cream
2 cups cooked wild rice
2 tablespoons minced fresh chervil, or 1 teaspoon
   crushed dried chervil
4 or 5 dashes bitters

Melt the butter in a heavy saucepan over medium heat. Add the onion, celery and carrot and sauté for 3 minutes. Reduce the heat and add the mushrooms. Sauté for 3 minutes. Sprinkle the flour, salt and white pepper over the vegetables and mix well. Cook until bubbly, stirring constantly.

Add the beef broth and milk and cook until thickened, stirring constantly. Add the wild rice, chervil and bitters. Simmer for 10 to 15 minutes or until of the desired consistency. Serve hot. Garnish servings with chopped celery tops or additional chopped carrots if desired.

Serves 10

Warrington Fish Chowder

3 or 4 medium potatoes, chopped
8 cups water
1/3 cup vegetable oil
2/3 cup all-purpose flour
1 large onion, chopped
1 large green bell pepper, chopped
2 garlic cloves, minced
1 (12-ounce) can tomato paste
2 pounds redfish, cut into bite-size pieces
1 lemon, cut into quarters
1 bay leaf
1 tablespoon salt
pepper to taste

Combine the potatoes and water in a large saucepan and bring to a boil. Reduce the heat and simmer while the roux is prepared.

Heat the vegetable oil in a skillet over medium-high heat. Stir in the flour and cook until medium brown, stirring constantly. Add the onion, bell pepper and garlic and cook until the onion is tender, stirring constantly. Remove from the heat and stir in the tomato paste.

Add the roux to the simmering potatoes. Add the fish, lemon, bay leaf, salt and pepper. Simmer for 10 to 30 minutes or until the potatoes are tender and the fish is cooked through. Discard the bay leaf and lemon quarters.

You may substitute grouper, snapper, sheephead or other firm fish for the redfish.

Serves 12

To an assortment of salad greens
add any of the following:

roasted walnuts, pecans,
sunflower seeds, pumpkin seeds
black beans
red onion
sliced mushrooms
blanched green beans
all colors of bell peppers
beets
chopped cucumber
shredded carrots
shoepeg corn
grape tomatoes
avocado
chopped celery
black and green olives
orange slices or mandarin oranges
fresh pineapple
golden raisins
grated fresh Parmesan cheese
feta cheese
crumbled crisp-cooked bacon
homemade croutons

To splurge add:

artichoke hearts
hearts of palm
blanched asparagus

Men's Secret Bleu Cheese Vinaigrette

2 or 3 garlic cloves, cut into halves
1/4 cup olive oil
2 tablespoons red wine vinegar with garlic
1 teaspoon chopped garlic
1/4 teaspoon sugar
1 teaspoon grated Parmesan cheese
1 teaspoon oregano flakes
1 teaspoon salt or seasoned salt
1 teaspoon coarsely ground pepper
1 tablespoon crumbled bleu cheese

Marinate the garlic cloves in the olive oil in a small bowl for 30 minutes; discard the garlic cloves.

Combine the vinegar, chopped garlic, sugar, Parmesan cheese, oregano flakes, seasoned salt and pepper in a bowl and mix well. Add the olive oil and mix well. Stir in the bleu cheese.

Pour into a container and store in the refrigerator. Shake before serving.

Makes 1/2 cup

Cilantro and Lime Vinaigrette

1 tablespoon fresh lime juice
1 tablespoon balsamic vinegar
1/3 cup buttermilk
1 tablespoon walnut oil or olive oil
1/4 cup chopped fresh cilantro
salt and pepper to taste

Whisk the lime juice and vinegar in a medium bowl until well blended. Whisk in the buttermilk, then the walnut oil and cilantro. Season with salt and pepper.

Cover and chill in the refrigerator for up to 6 hours.

Makes about 3/4 cup

Use the food being served as a focal point for inexpensive table decorating. Place empty baskets upside down and cover with cloths to support bread baskets on several levels, adding height and interest to the display. Mix in fresh fruit and cheeses for color and texture.

Sun-Dried Tomato Dressing

1 small red bell pepper
2 plum tomatoes, chopped
1 cup chopped onion
2 garlic cloves
1/4 teaspoon crushed dried red pepper
1 (8-ounce) jar oil-pack sun-dried tomatoes, drained and cut into strips
3/4 cup water
1/4 cup heavy cream
1/4 cup red wine vinegar
3 tablespoons fresh lemon juice
1/3 cup vegetable oil

Cut the bell pepper into halves and place cut side down on a baking sheet. Broil until the skin is blackened and blistered. Place in a paper bag and let stand for 10 minutes to loosen the skin. Remove and discard the skin; chop the pepper coarsely.

Combine the chopped bell pepper with the fresh tomatoes, onion, garlic and crushed red pepper in a food processor and process until smooth. Remove to a bowl.

Combine the sun-dried tomatoes, water, cream, vinegar and lemon juice in a food processor and process until smooth. Add the vegetable oil gradually, processing constantly until smooth.

Whisk the sun-dried tomato mixture into the fresh tomato mixture. Store in the refrigerator for up to 2 weeks.

Makes 3 1/2 cups

Olive Bread

1 envelope dry yeast
2 teaspoons sugar
1/2 cup warm (105- to 115-degree) water
1/2 cup cornmeal
1/2 cup chopped green olives
3/4 cup plain nonfat yogurt
1 tablespoon olive oil
1 teaspoon dried rosemary
3/4 teaspoon salt
3 cups bread flour

Dissolve the yeast and sugar in the warm water in a small bowl; let stand for 5 minutes. Combine with the cornmeal, olives, yogurt, olive oil, rosemary, salt and half the flour in a large mixing bowl. Beat at medium speed until well mixed. Add the remaining flour and mix to form a soft dough.

Knead on a lightly floured surface for 8 minutes or until smooth and elastic. Place in a large bowl sprayed with nonstick cooking spray, turning to coat the surface. Let rise, covered, in a sheltered 85-degree place for 1 hour or until doubled in bulk.

Punch down the dough and remove to a lightly floured surface. Let rest for 5 minutes. Knead lightly and roll into a 7×14-inch rectangle. Roll up from the short edge, pressing firmly to remove air pockets; pinch the seam and ends to seal.

Place seam side down in a 5×9-inch loaf pan sprayed with nonstick cooking spray. Let rise, covered, for 45 minutes or until doubled in bulk.

Bake at 375 degrees for 30 minutes or until the loaf sounds hollow when tapped. Remove from the pan immediately. Cool on a wire rack.

Makes 1 loaf

Red Pepper Cheese Bread

1 envelope dry yeast
2 teaspoons sugar
1 cup warm (105- to 115-degree) water
2 teaspoons Dijon mustard
1 tablespoon vegetable oil
1/2 teaspoon salt
1/4 to 1/2 teaspoon ground red pepper
3 cups bread flour
3/4 cup (6 ounces) shredded extra-sharp
   Cheddar cheese

Dissolve the yeast and sugar in the warm water in a large bowl; let stand for 5 minutes. Add the Dijon mustard, vegetable oil, salt, red pepper and 1 cup of the flour; mix until smooth. Add 1 3/4 cups flour and the cheese; stir to form a soft dough.

Knead the dough on a lightly floured surface for 10 minutes or until smooth and elastic, adding enough of the remaining flour 1 tablespoon at a time as necessary to prevent sticking.

Place the dough in a large bowl sprayed with nonstick cooking spray, turning to coat the surface. Let rise, covered, in a sheltered 85-degree place for 1 hour or until doubled in bulk. Punch down the dough and remove to a lightly floured surface. Roll up from the short edge, pressing firmly to remove air pockets; pinch the seam and ends to seal.

Place seam side down in a 5×9-inch loaf pan coated with nonstick cooking spray. Let rise, covered, for 1 hour or until doubled in bulk.

Bake at 375 degrees for 35 minutes or until the loaf sounds hollow when tapped. Remove from the pan immediately. Cool on a wire rack.

Makes 1 loaf

Cheesy Apple Pie

CHEESY PASTRY
1 cup all-purpose flour
1/4 teaspoon salt
1/3 cup butter-flavor shortening
1/2 cup (2 ounces) shredded Cheddar cheese
3 to 4 tablespoons cold water

APPLE FILLING
5 cups thinly sliced peeled cooking apples
1 cup sugar
1/4 cup all-purpose flour
1 teaspoon ground cinnamon
1/4 teaspoon salt

CHEDDAR CRUNCH TOPPING
3/4 cup each sugar and all-purpose flour
1/4 teaspoon salt
1/3 cup butter or margarine
1 cup (4 ounces) finely shredded Cheddar cheese

For the pastry, mix the flour and salt in a bowl. Cut in the shortening until crumbly. Stir in the cheese. Add enough cold water 1 tablespoon at a time to moisten, tossing with a fork to form a dough. Shape into a ball. Roll into a 12-inch circle on a lightly floured surface. Fit into a 9-inch pie plate and trim the edge to within 1/2 inch of the plate. Fold the edge under and flute.

For the filling, combine the apples, sugar, flour, cinnamon and salt in a bowl and toss to mix well. Spoon into the pastry.

For the topping, mix the sugar, flour and salt in a bowl. Cut in the butter until crumbly. Add the cheese and mix gently. Sprinkle over the filling. Cover the edge of the pastry with foil. Bake at 375 degrees for 25 minutes. Remove the foil and bake for 20 to 25 minutes longer or until the crust is golden brown and the apples are tender.

Serves 8

Chocolate Torte with Raspberry Sauce

CHOCOLATE TORTE
1 cup (6 ounces) chocolate chips
1 cup sugar
1 cup (2 sticks) unsalted butter, softened
8 large egg yolks
8 large egg whites, at room temperature

RASPBERRY SAUCE
2 (10-ounce) packages frozen raspberries in syrup, thawed
1/4 cup sugar
2 to 3 tablespoons orange liqueur

For the torte, melt the chocolate chips in a double boiler over boiling water. Combine the melted chocolate with the sugar and butter in a bowl and mix well. Cool to room temperature. Add the egg yolks 2 at a time, mixing well after each addition.

Beat the egg whites in a mixing bowl until stiff peaks form. Fold gently into the chocolate mixture. Spoon the batter into a buttered and floured 9-inch springform pan.

Bake at 325 degrees for 35 to 40 minutes or until a wooden pick inserted into the center comes out clean. Cool in the pan on a wire rack; the center of the torte will fall. Chill for 8 hours or longer.

For the sauce, drain the raspberries, reserving the juice from 1 package. Combine the raspberries, reserved juice, sugar and liqueur in a food processor and process until smooth. Strain into a bowl. Chill until serving time.

To serve, place the torte on a serving plate and remove the side of the pan. Cut into wedges with a hot knife. Serve with the raspberry sauce and garnish with sweetened whipped cream.

Serves 8 to 10

FIESTA BRUNCH FOR A BUNCH

Each spring, Pensacola celebrates "Fiesta of Five Flags" in tribute to the different governments that have counted her as their own: England, France, Spain, the Confederacy and the United States. Fiesta is a month long series of events including parades, parties and even a reenactment of Don Tristan de Luna's landing on the shores of the Gulf Coast. If your calendar is so full that breakfast is too early and lunch is too busy, try splitting the difference at mid-morning and enjoying a festive brunch. Happy Fiesta!

FRENCH ASPARAGUS AND MUSHROOM ROULADES
FRENCH COLD CUCUMBER SOUP
FRENCH ARTICHOKE QUICHE
AMERICAN SCRAMBLED EGGS WITH BACON AND TOMATO SAUCE
ENGLISH BEEF MEDALLIONS WITH CHERRY HORSERADISH SAUCE
CONFEDERATE COUNTRY GRITS AND SAUSAGE CASSEROLE
SPANISH SHRIMP AND ORANGE POTATO SALAD
RED-EYE GRAVY
AMERICAN GRILLED WHOLE TURKEY LOCO
AMERICAN CRANBERRY SALSA
SPANISH CONFETTI CORN TOSS
ENGLISH GINGER SCONES
CONFEDERATE PUMPKIN PRALINE PIE
SPANISH CHOCOLATE FLAN
ENGLISH TRIFLE
FRENCH POTS DE CRÈME
AMERICAN FROZEN BLOODY MARYS
CONFEDERATE LEMON MINT TEA
SPANISH SANGRIA
AMERICAN MINT JULEPS

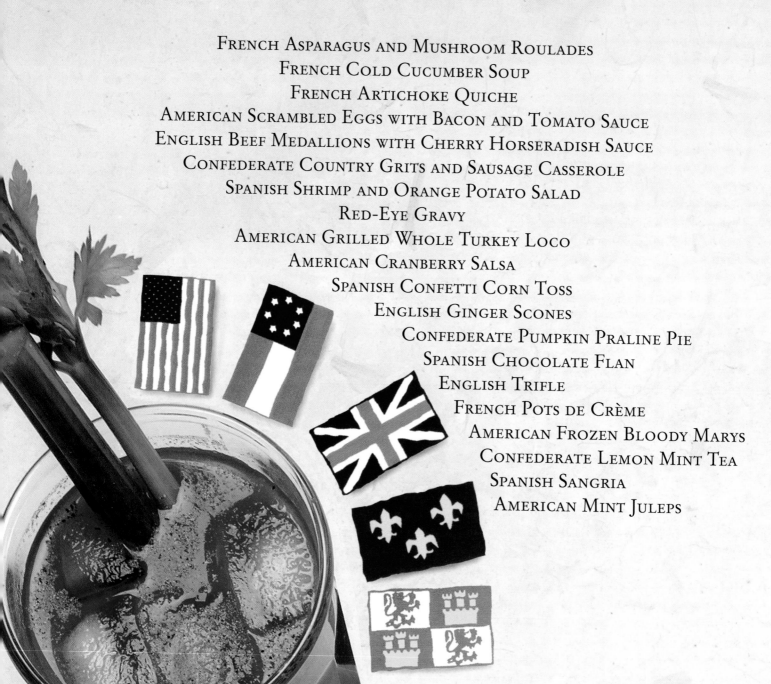

Celebrate Pensacola's Heritage
With a Fiesta Brunch
Featuring flavors from our past!

Sunday, June 8th
11:30 A.M.
Ferdinand Plaza

Sam & Newman Rodgers
RSVP   850-8505

French Asparagus and Mushroom Roulades

ASPARAGUS AND MUSHROOM FILLING
30 small or 18 large spears fresh asparagus
  (about 20 ounces)
1/2 teaspoon salt
1 tablespoon butter or margarine
1 pound fresh mushrooms, thinly sliced
1/2 teaspoon salt
1/2 teaspoon summer savory or thyme
2 teaspoons lemon juice
salt and pepper to taste

ROULADES
6 tablespoons seasoned bread crumbs
6 tablespoons finely chopped toasted walnuts
1/2 cup (1 stick) butter or margarine, melted
12 (12×17-inch) sheets fresh or thawed
  frozen phyllo
melted margarine
1 cup (4 ounces) plus 2 tablespoons shredded
  Gruyère or Swiss cheese

For the filling, trim the asparagus to 6-inch spears. Bring 1/2 inch water to a boil in a nonstick skillet over high heat. Add the asparagus and 1/2 teaspoon salt and return to a boil.

Reduce the heat to medium-low and cook, covered, for 4 to 8 minutes or until the asparagus is tender. Remove the asparagus to a bowl, drain and wipe out the skillet.

Melt the butter in the skillet over medium-high heat. Add the mushrooms, 1/2 teaspoon salt and seasoning. Cook until the mushrooms are brown and the liquid evaporates. Add the lemon juice and cook for 30 seconds longer. Add salt and pepper to taste. Remove the mushrooms to a bowl and cool to room temperature.

For the roulades, mix the bread crumbs and walnuts in a small bowl. Add 1/2 cup melted butter and mix well.

For the assembly, place one phyllo sheet on a work surface with the short side toward you; keep the remaining phyllo covered to prevent drying out.

Brush the phyllo with melted margarine and sprinkle with about 2 tablespoons of the walnut-crumb mixture. Top with a second phyllo sheet and brush with melted margarine. Sprinkle 3 tablespoons of the cheese in a strip 2 inches from the short edge, leaving a 11/2-inch border on either side.

Arrange 5 small or 3 large asparagus spears on the cheese. Divide the mushrooms into 6 equal portions and top the asparagus with one portion of mushrooms. Roll the phyllo to enclose the filling, folding in the sides. Place seam side down on a lightly greased baking sheet. Brush lightly with melted margarine.

Repeat the procedure with the remaining ingredients. Bake at 375 degrees for 25 minutes or until puffed and golden brown. Garnish with fresh herbs. Serve immediately.

Serves 6

You may choose to group the food for the Fiesta Brunch by country on the buffet table, using miniature flags and flowers to designate each section. Seat guests at tables covered with white tablecloths and draped with the colors of the five flags.

French Cold Cucumber Soup

2 cucumbers
2 cups chicken broth
1 onion, chopped
1 teaspoon dried dillweed
salt and pepper to taste
2 cups plain yogurt

Peel and seed the cucumbers and cut into strips. Combine the cucumber strips with the chicken broth and onion in a saucepan. Cook over low heat until the cucumbers and onion are tender. Process in a blender until the mixture is smooth. Remove to a bowl and season with the dillweed, salt and pepper. Cool to room temperature.

Add the yogurt and mix gently. Chill until serving time. Garnish servings with cucumber slices and sprigs of fresh dill.

Serves 4 to 6

French Artichoke Quiche

1 unbaked (9-inch) pastry shell
1/3 cup chopped green onions
2 tablespoons butter, melted
2 eggs
1 tablespoon all-purpose flour
2/3 cup light cream
1 (14-ounce) can artichoke hearts, drained and chopped
1 cup (4 ounces) shredded sharp Cheddar cheese
1 cup (4 ounces) shredded hot pepper cheese

Prick the pastry shell with a fork and bake at 400 degrees for 12 minutes. Remove the shell from the oven and reduce the oven temperature to 350 degrees.

Sauté the green onions in the butter in a skillet. Combine the eggs, flour and cream in a mixing bowl and beat until smooth. Stir in the sautéed green onions and artichokes.

Reserve 3 tablespoons of the Cheddar cheese. Stir the remaining Cheddar cheese and the pepper cheese into the artichoke mixture. Spoon into the pastry shell. Bake for 35 minutes. Sprinkle with the reserved cheese. Bake for 10 minutes longer or until a knife inserted in the center comes out clean.

Serves 4 to 6

American Scrambled Eggs with Bacon and Tomato Sauce

6 slices bacon
1/2 cup olive oil
1 large onion, chopped
2 tablespoons minced garlic
2 (16-ounce) cans diced tomatoes
1/4 cup chopped fresh basil
1/4 cup red wine
1 teaspoon chopped parsley
1 teaspoon hot sauce
salt and pepper to taste
8 eggs, beaten
1 tablespoon butter

Cook the bacon in a skillet until crisp. Drain and crumble the bacon. Drain most of the drippings from the skillet. Add the olive oil to the skillet and heat over medium heat. Add the onion and sauté until translucent. Add the garlic and cook for 2 minutes, stirring constantly.

Stir in the tomatoes, basil, wine, parsley, hot sauce, salt and pepper. Cook over medium heat for 15 minutes. Reduce the heat and simmer for 20 minutes longer.

Scramble the eggs in the butter in a nonstick skillet until soft-set. Season with salt and pepper. Remove to a platter and sprinkle with the crumbled bacon. Serve with the tomato sauce.

The tomato sauce is also good served over hot cooked spaghetti and topped with freshly grated Parmesan cheese.

Serves 4

English Beef Medallions with Cherry Horseradish Sauce

2 pounds beef tenderloin or beef tips
1/2 cup cranberry juice
1/4 cup unbleached flour
2 teaspoons thyme
salt and coarsely ground pepper to taste
2 tablespoons butter
2 tablespoons olive oil
1/4 cup bourbon
1 1/4 cups beef stock
1/2 cup cranberry juice
1/2 cup sun-dried cherries
2 tablespoons horseradish

Cut the beef into 1/2-inch pieces. Combine with 1/2 cup cranberry juice in a bowl and marinate for 1 hour. Drain, discarding the marinade. Pat the beef dry.

Mix the flour, thyme, salt and pepper in a bowl or sealable plastic bag. Add the beef and mix or shake to coat well. Sauté the beef in the butter and olive oil in a skillet until medium rare or until done to taste. Remove to a bowl.

Add the bourbon to the skillet, stirring to deglaze the bottom. Cook until the liquid is reduced by 1/2. Add the beef stock, 1/2 cup cranberry juice, sun-dried cherries and horseradish and mix well. Cook until heated through. Pour over the beef and serve immediately.

Serves 8

Confederate Country Grits and Sausage Casserole

2 pounds mild bulk pork sausage
4 cups water
1¹/4 cups uncooked grits
4 cups (16 ounces) shredded sharp Cheddar
  cheese
1 cup milk
¹/8 teaspoon garlic powder
¹/2 teaspoon dried thyme
4 eggs, beaten
paprika to taste

Brown the sausage in a large skillet, stirring until crumbly; drain.

Bring the water to a boil in a saucepan. Stir in the grits and return to a boil. Reduce the heat and cover. Cook until the water is absorbed and the grits are thickened.

Remove from the heat and add the Cheddar cheese, milk, garlic powder and thyme; stir until the cheese melts. Stir in the sausage and eggs.

Spoon into a lightly greased 9×13-inch baking dish. Sprinkle with paprika and bake at 350 degrees for 1 hour or until golden brown and set. Let stand for 5 minutes before serving.

You may prepare the casserole in advance and store in the refrigerator. Let stand, covered, at room temperature for 30 minutes before baking.

Serves 8 to 10

Spanish Shrimp and Orange Potato Salad

2 seedless oranges
6 small red potatoes
12 small pimento-stuffed green olives
3 tablespoons red wine vinegar
6 tablespoons vegetable oil or olive oil
hot pepper sauce to taste
salt to taste
18 shrimp, cooked, peeled and deveined

Grate the zest from the oranges. Peel the oranges and separate into sections; cut each section into 3 pieces.

Cook the unpeeled potatoes in water to cover in a saucepan until tender; drain. Cut into 1-inch pieces.

Combine the olives, vinegar, vegetable oil, hot sauce and salt in a bowl and mix well. Add the shrimp, orange pieces, orange zest and potatoes and mix to coat well. Chill until serving time.

Serves 6

RED-EYE GRAVY

Reserve the drippings from baking a country ham. Pour off or chill and remove the fat from the drippings. Combine the drippings with 4 cups hot strong brewed coffee and ¹/2 cup packed brown sugar in the pan used to bake the ham, stirring to deglaze the bottom. Cook for 15 minutes or until reduced by half, stirring occasionally. Serve with the country ham.

American Grilled Whole Turkey Loco

1 (12-pound) turkey
1/2 cup (1 stick) butter
juice of 6 limes
2 tablespoons tequila
2 tablespoons finely chopped fresh oregano, or
    1 teaspoon dried oregano
salt and freshly ground pepper to taste
American Cranberry Salsa (at right)

Ask the butcher to butterfly the turkey, discarding the excess skin and fat. Rinse the turkey and pat dry; insert a meat thermometer into the thickest portion, not touching the bone.

Melt the butter in a saucepan. Stir in the lime juice, tequila, oregano, salt and pepper. Place the turkey cut side up on an oiled grill 6 inches from the heat source. Brush with the lime mixture and grill for 15 minutes. Turn the turkey and brush with additional lime mixture.

Grill for a total of 1 1/2 to 2 hours or to 170 degrees on the meat thermometer, turning every 20 minutes and brushing with the lime mixture. Serve with American Cranberry Salsa.

Serves 16

First celebrated in 1959, Pensacola's annual Fiesta of Five Flags is one of the oldest and largest festivals in Florida. It celebrates the landing of Spanish Conquistador Don Tristan de Luna and the subsequent occupations by the French, British, United States, and Confederacy. The street names in Pensacola reflect the various occupations, with 155 of Spanish origin, 57 of English origin, and 51 of French origin.

American Cranberry Salsa

2 cups fresh cranberries or thawed frozen
    cranberries
4 teaspoons grated orange zest
chopped sections of 2 large oranges
1/4 cup chopped onion
1 tablespoon minced fresh coriander
1 tablespoon minced fresh gingerroot
1 tablespoon minced seeded jalapeño pepper
salt to taste

Process the cranberries in a food processor until coarsely chopped. Combine with the orange zest, orange sections, onion, coriander, gingerroot, jalapeño pepper and salt in a bowl and mix well.

Let stand for 30 minutes or longer to blend the flavors. Serve at room temperature.

Makes 4 cups

Spanish Confetti Corn Toss

2 (16-ounce) cans whole kernel corn, drained
1 (15-ounce) can black beans, rinsed and drained
1 (14-ounce) can hearts of palm, drained and sliced
2 large tomatoes, seeded and chopped
1/2 cup chopped purple onion
1/3 cup minced fresh cilantro
1/4 cup vegetable oil
3 tablespoons lime juice
1 1/2 teaspoons chili powder
1/2 teaspoon ground cumin

Combine the corn, beans, hearts of palm, tomatoes, onion and cilantro in a large bowl and mix gently. Combine the vegetable oil, lime juice, chili powder and cumin in a small bowl and mix well. Add to the vegetable mixture and mix gently. Chill, covered, for 3 hours or longer. Garnish with fresh cilantro sprigs and tortilla chips.

Serves 8

English Ginger Scones

2 1/4 cups all-purpose flour
1/3 cup sugar
1 tablespoon baking powder
1/4 teaspoon grated lemon zest
1/2 cup (1 stick) plus 3 tablespoons unsalted butter, chilled and chopped
3/4 cup heavy cream
2/3 cup finely chopped candied ginger
2 tablespoons heavy cream

Combine the flour, sugar, baking powder and lemon zest in a food processor and process to mix well. Add the butter and pulse until the mixture resembles coarse cornmeal. Remove to a large bowl and make a well in the center. Add 3/4 cup cream and stir with a fork just until moistened. Mix in the ginger.

Knead on a floured surface for 8 minutes or until smooth. Divide into 2 equal portions and pat each into a circle 3/4 inch thick. Cut each circle into 6 wedges.

Place 1 inch apart on a lightly buttered baking sheet. Brush the tops with 2 tablespoons cream. Bake at 400 degrees for 18 minutes. Serve warm.

You may freeze baked scones in airtight sealable plastic bags, thaw in the refrigerator and rewarm in a 350-degree oven.

Makes 1 dozen

Confederate Pumpkin Praline Pie

PIE

3 eggs
2/3 cup sugar
2 cups fresh or canned cooked pumpkin purée
1 1/4 cups half-and-half
3 tablespoons bourbon
1/2 teaspoon grated fresh nutmeg
1/2 teaspoon ground ginger
1/2 teaspoon allspice
1/8 teaspoon salt
Pecan Pastry (page 31)

PECAN TOPPING

3/4 cup packed brown sugar
1/4 cup (1/2 stick) unsalted butter, melted
2 tablespoons heavy cream
2/3 cup coarsely chopped pecans
1/2 cup pecan halves
1/2 cup whipping cream
1 teaspoon vanilla extract

For the pie, combine the eggs and sugar in a mixing bowl or food processor and beat or process for 3 minutes or until thick and lemon-colored. Add the pumpkin, half-and-half, bourbon, nutmeg, ginger, allspice and salt and mix well.

Don Tristan de Luna y Arrelano, with 1500 would-be settlers and soldiers, made the first attempt to colonize Pensacola Bay in 1559, making it the oldest colony in America. He named the bay Bahia Santa Maria de Filipina, but the colony was destroyed after only two years.

Spoon into the prepared pastry shell. Bake at 400 degrees for 15 minutes. Reduce the oven temperature to 350 degrees and bake for 35 to 45 minutes longer or until set. Cool to room temperature on a wire rack.

For the topping, combine the brown sugar, butter, 2 tablespoons heavy cream and chopped pecans in a bowl and mix well. Spread over the pie. Arrange the pecan halves over the top. Broil just until the topping is brown, turning to brown evenly.

Whip 1/2 cup whipping cream in a mixing bowl until soft peaks form. Add the vanilla and mix well. Spoon over servings.

Serves 6 to 8

Pecan Pastry

1 1/2 cups pastry flour
1 tablespoon confectioners' sugar
1/8 teaspoon salt
1 tablespoon coarsely chopped pecans
9 tablespoons (1 stick plus 1 tablespoon) unsalted
    butter, frozen and chopped
1/4 cup cold water

Combine the flour, confectioners' sugar, salt and
pecans in a food processor and process for a few
seconds to mix well. Add the butter and process
for 5 to 10 seconds or until the mixture resembles
coarse meal. Add the water gradually, processing
constantly just until the mixture sticks together
when pinched.

Press into a disk on a lightly floured pastry board.
Roll into a circle large enough to fit into a 9-inch
pie pan, 11-inch tart pan with a removable bottom
or 11-inch flan ring placed on a baking sheet.
Drape the dough over the rolling pin and remove
to the pan. Place the tart pan or pie pan on a
baking sheet and press the pastry against the side,
pressing to extend over the rim of a pie pan or
1/4 to 1/2 inch above the rim of a tart pan.

Cover with baking parchment or foil and press
to fit smoothly. Fill with pie weights, dried beans
or rice. Bake at 400 degrees for 8 minutes. Remove
the pie weights and parchment and prick the
pastry. Bake for 5 minutes longer. Cool on a wire
rack for 15 minutes.

Makes 1 pie shell

Spanish Chocolate Flan

10 tablespoons sugar
5 tablespoons water
1 cup milk
1 cup (6 ounces) semisweet chocolate chips
1 1/2 cups milk
3 eggs
3 egg yolks
6 tablespoons packed light brown sugar

Combine the sugar and the water in a skillet.
Cook until the mixture is caramelized and golden
brown. Pour immediately into a shallow 6-cup
baking dish.

Heat 1 cup milk in a small saucepan and add the
chocolate chips, stirring to melt the chocolate.
Remove from the heat and stir in 1 1/2 cups milk.
Cool to room temperature, stirring occasionally.

Combine the eggs, egg yolks and brown sugar
in a mixing bowl and beat until smooth. Add the
chocolate mixture and mix well. Pour into the
baking dish.

Place the baking dish into a larger pan and add
enough water to reach halfway up the side of the
dish. Bake at 350 degrees for 45 minutes or until
the center is set. Cool on a wire rack. Invert onto
a serving plate and slice into wedges to serve,
spooning the caramel sauce over each serving.

You may also bake the flan in individual ramekins.

Serves 6 to 8

English Trifle

1 (12-ounce) pound cake
1/2 cup sweet sherry or fruit liqueur (optional)
chopped or sliced and seeded fresh fruit in season
2 cups vanilla custard
2 cups whipping cream, whipped
1 cup toasted almond halves

Line the bottom of a trifle bowl or glass bowl with half the cake slices. Brush with half the sherry. Layer half the fruit, custard, whipped cream and almonds over the cake. Repeat the layers with the remaining cake, sherry, custard and whipped cream. Garnish with additional fruit. Serve immediately or chill for several hours.

Serves 8

French Pots de Crème

1 cup (6 ounces) semisweet chocolate chips or
    mint chocolate chips
2 tablespoons sugar
1 egg
1 teaspoon vanilla extract
1/8 teaspoon salt
3/4 cup milk

Combine the chocolate chips, sugar, egg, vanilla and salt in a blender. Bring the milk to a boil in a saucepan. Pour into the blender and process for 1 minute or until the chocolate melts. Pour immediately into ramekins. Chill until serving time. Garnish with whipped cream.

Serves 4 or 5

American Frozen Bloody Marys

1/2 cup tomato juice
1 cup chopped tomato, frozen
1/4 cup vodka
1 tablespoon fresh lemon juice
4 teaspoons Worcestershire sauce
hot pepper sauce to taste
1/4 teaspoon salt
freshly ground pepper to taste
1 1/2 cups small ice cubes

Combine the tomato juice, frozen tomato, vodka, lemon juice, Worcestershire sauce, hot sauce, salt, pepper and ice cubes in a blender and process until smooth. Pour into glasses. Garnish with skewers of cherry tomatoes, fresh basil and mozzarella cubes.

Serves 2

Spanish Sangria

1 lemon
1 orange
1/2 cup sugar
1/2 cup water
1 (750-milliliter) bottle of dry red wine, chilled
3 tablespoons brandy
1 1/2 cups club soda, chilled

Cut the lemon and orange into 1/4-inch slices.
Combine 2 lemon slices and 2 orange slices with
the sugar and water in a saucepan. Bring to a boil
and cook until the sugar dissolves, stirring
constantly. Cool to room temperature.

Press the lemon and orange slices in the sugar
syrup to release the juice; discard the slices.
Combine the syrup with the remaining sliced fruit,
wine, brandy and club soda in a pitcher and mix
gently. Serve over ice in glasses.

Serves 12

American Mint Juleps

3/4 cup sugar
1 cup water
50 fresh mint leaves
5 cups bourbon

Combine the sugar and water in a small saucepan
and heat over low heat for 20 minutes or until the
sugar dissolves completely, stirring constantly. Cool
to room temperature.

Add the mint leaves to the sugar syrup and crush
with the back of a spoon. Let stand for 2 hours;
strain. Store in the refrigerator indefinitely.

To serve, pour about 1 tablespoon of the mint
syrup into ice-filled glasses. Pour about 1/4 cup
bourbon into each glass and stir to mix. Garnish
with fresh mint sprigs.

Serves 20

Elegant Entertaining

Elegance does not have to mean expensive and certainly does not mean extravagant. Indeed, tasteful restraint and grace characterize true elegance. In this section, ordinary occasions are made extraordinary by combining the right mix of food, wine and creative ambience.

MESSAGES IN A BOTTLE

SEEING RED

FEAST FROM THE LODGE

No Wake Zone

© Paul Jackson

MESSAGES IN A BOTTLE

*Imagine a close group of family and friends gathering to celebrate the recent engagement
of a special couple. Each guest bears a gift—a bottle filled with the finest wine.
Tied around the neck of each bottle is a message written especially for the bride and groom.
A message of hope, encouragement or practical advice. Or perhaps a simple wish.
It's the perfect opportunity to turn an already happy occasion into a unique and elegant gathering.*

SHERRIED ONIONS AND OLIVES

MINIATURE SPINACH SALADS IN PHYLLO SHELLS

GRIT CAKES WITH SHRIMP

CRAB FINGERS IN CITRUS VINAIGRETTE

PEPPERCORN PASTRIES WITH BEEF AND HORSERADISH CREAM

STRAWBERRIES WITH CRÈME FRAÎCHE

PANNA COTTA WITH RASPBERRY SAUCE

Sherried Onions and Olives

1/2 cup dry sherry
1/4 cup red wine vinegar
2 tablespoons vegetable oil
1 garlic clove, minced
1/2 teaspoon each crushed dried oregano and basil
1 cup frozen small whole onions, thawed
1 (6-ounce) can pitted black olives, drained
1 (2 1/2-ounce) jar pimento-stuffed olives, drained

Mix the first 6 ingredients in a bowl. Add the onions and olives and mix gently. Cover and chill for 1 to 3 days, stirring occasionally. Remove to a serving dish with a slotted spoon.

Serves 10 to 12

ORANGE MARTINI

Combine 2 ounces orange vodka, 3/4 ounce Grand Marnier and 1 1/2 ounces orange juice with 1/3 cup crushed ice in a martini shaker. Shake gently for 10 seconds. Pour into a chilled glass.

Miniature Spinach Salads in Phyllo Shells

DIJON VINAIGRETTE

2 teaspoons white or red wine vinegar, sherry vinegar, balsamic vinegar or fresh lemon juice
1/2 teaspoon Dijon mustard
salt to taste
2 tablespoons extra-virgin olive oil
pepper to taste

SPINACH SALAD

1 cup packed tiny spinach leaves or torn large spinach leaves, stems removed
2 tablespoons finely crumbled Roquefort or other bleu cheese
2 slices smoked bacon, crisp-cooked and crumbled
2 tablespoons finely chopped red onion
24 miniature phyllo shells

For the vinaigrette, combine the vinegar, Dijon mustard and salt in a small bowl. Add the olive oil gradually, whisking constantly until smooth. Season with pepper.

For the salad, stack several spinach leaves at a time and roll up from the stem end. Cut into very thin slices with a sharp knife. Combine the spinach with the Roquefort cheese, bacon and onion in a bowl. Drizzle with the vinaigrette and toss lightly to coat.

Spoon 1 scant tablespoon of the salad into each phyllo shell. You may also serve the salad on crackers.

Makes 24

Grit Cakes with Shrimp

GRITS AND SHRIMP
12 medium shrimp
6 cups water
2¹/2 cups uncooked grits
2 cups (8 ounces) shredded Cheddar cheese
¹/2 cup minced white and pale green portions of
    scallions
1 tablespoon ground cumin
2 teaspoons salt
1¹/2 teaspoons white pepper
¹/2 teaspoon cayenne pepper

GRIT CAKES
¹/2 cup all-purpose flour
¹/2 cup cornmeal
2 tablespoons (or more) butter
2 tablespoons vegetable oil
¹/2 cup pepper jelly

To prepare the shrimp and grits, bring a medium saucepan of water to a boil. Add the shrimp and cook for 1 to 2 minutes or until opaque. Remove to a large bowl of ice water to cool. Peel the shrimp and cut into halves lengthwise, discarding the veins.

Bring 6 cups water to a boil in a medium saucepan. Sprinkle the grits gradually into the boiling water, whisking constantly. Reduce the heat to medium and cook for 5 to 7 minutes or until thick, whisking constantly. Remove from the heat and stir in the Cheddar cheese, scallions, cumin, salt, white pepper and cayenne pepper.

Pour into a buttered 10×15-inch pan and spread into a ¹/2-inch layer. Mark 24 circles in the grits by pressing lightly with a 2¹/2-inch round cookie cutter. Press 1 shrimp half into each circle. Cover with plastic wrap, press down lightly and chill for 1 to 2 hours or until set.

For the cakes, mix the flour and cornmeal in a small bowl. Cut the grits along the marked lines with a cookie cutter, keeping the shrimp centered in each circle. Coat the cakes with the flour mixture.

Heat 2 teaspoons butter and 2 teaspoons vegetable oil at a time in a large skillet over medium-high heat. Sauté the cakes 8 at a time in the skillet for 1 to 2 minutes on each side or until golden brown, wiping out the skillet and adding additional butter and vegetable oil between batches; press any shrimp that loosen back into the cakes as they cook.

Top the grit cakes with the pepper jelly and garnish with scallion greens. Serve warm.

Makes 24

Crab Fingers in Citrus Vinaigrette

¹/2 cup freshly squeezed orange juice
¹/2 cup freshly squeezed ruby red grapefruit juice
¹/4 cup raspberry vinegar
¹/2 cup olive oil
salt and pepper to taste
1 pound jumbo crab fingers (or claws)

Whisk the orange juice, ruby red grapefruit juice, raspberry vinegar and olive oil together in a bowl. Season with salt and pepper. Add the crab fingers and marinate for 45 minutes. Drain excess marinade and arrange the crab fingers on a serving platter to serve.

Serves 6

Peppercorn Pastries with Beef and Horseradish Cream

1 sheet frozen puff pastry, thawed
1 egg, lightly beaten
1 teaspoon water
Horseradish Cream (at right)
8 ounces medium-rare beef tenderloin, chilled and thinly sliced (at right), or very thinly sliced deli beef, cut into 1¹/2-inch strips
1 teaspoon cracked pepper
assorted fresh herbs

Unfold the puff pastry on a lightly floured work surface and roll to a 10×15-inch rectangle. Cut the rectangle crosswise into strips 1¹/2 inches wide; cut the strips crosswise into thirds. Place about 1 inch apart on 2 ungreased baking sheets. Blend the egg and water in a bowl and brush over the pastry strips.

Bake the pastry at 375 degrees for 8 to 10 minutes or until light brown. Remove to a wire rack to cool completely.

Spread about 2 teaspoons Horseradish Cream on each pastry, leaving a small border. Arrange 1 slice of beef accordion-style on each pastry. Sprinkle with pepper and fresh herbs. Arrange on a serving platter.

For a picnic, pack the Horseradish Cream and the beef and pastry in separate containers in an insulated cooler and assemble just before serving.

Makes 30

BEEF TENDERLOIN

To roast a 2- to 2¹/2-pound beef tenderloin roast for Peppercorn Pastries with Beef and Horseradish Cream, place the roast on a rack in a shallow roasting pan and insert a meat thermometer into the thickest portion. Roast, uncovered, at 425 degrees for 30 to 45 minutes or to 140 degrees on the meat thermometer. Cover and let stand at room temperature until cool. Chill, covered, in the refrigerator. Cut into very thin slices to serve.

Horseradish Cream

8 ounces sour cream
2 tablespoons mixed chopped fresh herbs, such as basil, oregano, thyme, dill and/or parsley
4 teaspoons prepared horseradish
1 tablespoon milk
1 garlic clove, minced

Combine the sour cream, fresh herbs, horseradish, milk and garlic in a small bowl and mix well. Chill, covered, for up to 24 hours.

Makes 1¹/4 cups

Strawberries with Crème Fraîche

CRÈME FRAÎCHE
1/4 cup heavy cream
1/4 cup sour cream

STRAWBERRIES
18 large or 24 medium strawberries
8 ounces cream cheese, softened
1/4 cup sifted confectioners' sugar
1 tablespoon finely chopped toasted almonds

For the crème fraîche, combine the cream and sour cream in a bowl and mix well. Cover with plastic wrap and let stand at room temperature for 2 to 5 hours or until thickened. Store, covered, in the refrigerator for up to 1 week. Stir before using.

For the strawberries, gently rinse and hull the berries and pat dry with paper towels. Place each strawberry stem end down on a work surface and slice each 3 times cutting to, but not through, the stem end. Fan out the slices slightly.

Beat the cream cheese and confectioner's sugar at medium speed in a small mixing bowl until smooth. Stir the crème fraîche and fold 1/4 cup into the cream cheese mixture. Spoon into a decorating bag fitted with a medium star or round tip with a 1/4-inch opening. Pipe into each strawberry. Sprinkle with the almonds. Chill until serving time.

You may substitute Medjool dates for the strawberries if preferred. Cut a lengthwise slit in each date and remove the pit before filling with the cream cheese mixture. Do not use ultrapasturized whipping cream for the crème fraîche; store unused crème fraîche in the refrigerator for up to 1 week.

Makes 18 to 24

Panna Cotta with Raspberry Sauce

PANNA COTTA
4 teaspoons unflavored gelatin
1/4 cup cold water
4 cups heavy cream
1 cup sugar
1/4 teaspoon vanilla extract

RASPBERRY SAUCE
4 cups raspberries
1/2 cup sugar

For the panna cotta, sprinkle the gelatin over the cold water in a metal mixing bowl or double boiler and let stand for 10 minutes or until the gelatin softens. Place the bowl or double boiler over boiling water and heat for 1 minute or until the gelatin dissolves completely, stirring constantly.

Combine the cream, sugar and vanilla in a large heavy saucepan. Bring to a boil and cook until the sugar dissolves, stirring constantly. Add the gelatin mixture and whisk to blend well.

Spoon into ten 3/4-cup custard cups. Chill for 8 hours or longer.

For the raspberry sauce, combine the raspberries and sugar in a food processor and process to mix well.

To serve, place the custard cups in a shallow pan of warm water for 20 seconds or until loosened. Invert onto serving plates and top with the raspberry sauce.

Serves 10

SEEING RED

*While the South is not considered wine country, we enjoy the sampling, choosing and pairing of
wines with our favorite foods. Of course, we do know a great deal about throwing an elegant party,
and there's something about the fruit of the vine that lends elegance to any occasion.
Invite your favorite connoisseur to join your friends for an evening of wine tasting.
You can review the basics of wine selection and, more importantly,
enjoy your favorites with an interesting mix of delicious appetizers.*

MEDITERRANEAN TOMATO BITES
BLEU CHEESE PECAN GRAPES
ROASTED EGGPLANT SPREAD
FRUIT AND CHEESE TRAY
CROSTINI WITH ROASTED PEPPER SPREAD
MARINATED SHRIMP ON ROSEMARY SKEWERS
ROASTED POTATOES WITH FRESH TOMATO AND
AVOCADO SALSA
PEACHES IN WINE
ORANGE TIRAMISU

Seeing Red...
You will be!

Join us for a Wine Tasting
Saturday, October 12th
6:00 P.M.
31 Cabernet Drive

The Jacobis

850-WINE

Mediterranean Tomato Bites

12 small plum tomatoes
3/4 cup cooked acini di pepe or orzo
1/2 (6-ounce) jar marinated artichoke hearts,
    drained and chopped
2 tablespoons thinly sliced green onions
2 tablespoons finely chopped red or
    yellow bell pepper
2 tablespoons chopped golden raisins
2 tablespoons chopped toasted pine nuts
2 tablespoons crumbled bleu cheese or feta cheese
2 tablespoons olive oil
2 tablespoons white wine vinegar
2 teaspoons chopped fresh basil, or
    1/4 teaspoon crushed dried basil
1/4 teaspoon salt
1/4 teaspoon pepper

Cut the tomatoes into halves lengthwise. Scoop out and discard the seeds and pulp, leaving shells 1/4 inch thick. Place cut side down on paper towels and let stand for 30 minutes.

Combine the pasta, artichoke hearts, green onions, bell pepper, raisins, pine nuts and bleu cheese in a bowl and mix well. Stir in the olive oil, vinegar, basil, salt and pepper.

Spoon the pasta mixture into the tomato shells and arrange on a serving platter. Chill, covered, until serving time.

You may substitute cherry tomatoes for the plum tomatoes. Cut a slice off the top of each to scoop out the pulp and cut a thin slice from the bottom if necessary to help them stand upright.

Makes 24

BLEU CHEESE PECAN GRAPES

Combine 4 ounces crumbled bleu cheese with 3 ounces softened cream cheese in a small mixing bowl and beat at medium speed until smooth. Chill for 1 hour or longer. Discard the stems from 4 ounces seedless grapes and wash the grapes; pat completely dry. Shape a small amount of the cheese mixture around each grape, enclosing completely. Roll in 1 cup finely chopped toasted pecans, coating well. Chill for 1 hour or longer.

Roasted Eggplant Spread

1 medium eggplant, peeled, cut into 1-inch pieces
2 red bell peppers, seeded, cut into 1-inch pieces
1 red onion, cut into 1-inch pieces
2 garlic cloves, minced
3 tablespoons olive oil
1 1/2 teaspoons kosher salt
1/2 teaspoon freshly ground pepper
1 tablespoon tomato paste

Combine the eggplant, bell peppers, onion, garlic, olive oil, kosher salt and pepper in a large bowl and toss to coat evenly. Spread on a baking sheet. Roast at 400 degrees for 45 minutes or until the vegetables are light brown and tender, tossing once; cool. Remove the vegetables to a food processor and add the tomato paste. Pulse 3 or 4 times to mix well. Adjust the seasonings. Serve with pita bread.

Serves 6 to 8

Crostini with Roasted Pepper Spread

ROASTED PEPPER SPREAD
1 small onion, finely chopped
1 tablespoon olive oil
1 (12-ounce) jar or 2 (7-ounce) jars roasted red peppers, drained
1 (7-ounce) can diced tomatoes
1 teaspoon fennel seeds, crushed
1/2 teaspoon sugar
1/4 teaspoon salt
1/4 teaspoon pepper

CROSTINI
1 (12-ounce) baguette
1/2 cup olive oil
2 tablespoons finely chopped fresh basil
garlic powder to taste
1/2 teaspoon lemon pepper

For the roasted pepper spread, sauté the onion in the olive oil in a 10-inch skillet until tender but not brown. Add the roasted red peppers, undrained tomatoes, fennel seeds, sugar, salt and pepper and mix well. Bring to a boil and reduce the heat. Simmer for 10 minutes or until most of the liquid has evaporated.

Cool the mixture slightly. Process in a blender until smooth. Remove to a bowl and chill, covered, for up to 4 days.

For the crostini, cut the baguette into 1/4-inch slices. Arrange in a single layer on a baking sheet. Combine the olive oil, basil, garlic powder and lemon pepper in a small bowl. Brush on 1 side of each bread slice. Broil 3 to 4 inches from the heat source for 2 minutes or until toasted. Turn the slices and broil for 1 to 2 minutes longer or until golden brown. Cool to room temperature. Store in an airtight container.

To serve, let the pepper spread stand at room temperature for 30 minutes. Serve with the toasted crostini.

You may also serve the crostini with Roasted Red Bell Pepper Sauce (below).

Makes 30

Roasted Red Bell Pepper Sauce

2 medium red bell peppers, or 1 (7-ounce) jar roasted red bell peppers
1 large tomato
1/2 cup red wine vinegar
3/4 cup olive oil
1 cup water
6 garlic cloves
30 blanched almonds, toasted
salt to taste
Crostini (at left)

Cut the bell peppers into halves and place cut side down on a baking sheet. Roast at 450 degrees until evenly charred. Place in a paper bag and seal; let stand for 10 minutes. Remove the skin under running water. Chop the peppers.

Immerse the tomato in boiling water in a saucepan for 30 to 60 seconds or until the skin will slip off easily. Chop the tomato. Combine the roasted peppers, tomato, vinegar, olive oil, water, garlic, almonds and salt in a food processor and process until coarsely chopped. Serve at room temperature with the crostini.

You may also serve this sauce with asparagus and other fresh vegetables or with shrimp, fish and meat.

Makes 3 cups

Marinated Shrimp on Rosemary Skewers

ROSEMARY MARINADE
1/2 cup extra-virgin olive oil
1 tablespoon ketchup
1 teaspoon chopped fresh rosemary
4 garlic cloves, minced
8 whole black peppercorns

SHRIMP
24 jumbo shrimp, peeled and deveined,
   about 2 pounds
8 (8-inch) rosemary stems or bamboo skewers
2 medium zucchini

For the marinade, combine the olive oil, ketchup, rosemary, garlic and peppercorns in a bowl and mix well.

For the shrimp, add the shrimp to the marinade and toss to coat well. Marinate, covered, at room temperature for 30 minutes or in the refrigerator for 4 hours or longer.

Soak the rosemary stems or skewers in water to cover in a bowl for 30 minutes or longer. Slice the zucchini diagonally into sixteen 1/2-inch pieces. Drain the stems and shrimp. Thread 3 shrimp onto each stem alternately with 2 zucchini pieces, leaving 1/4 inch between each.

Place on a greased rack and grill over medium heat for 10 to 14 minutes or until the shrimp are pink and opaque, turning occasionally.

Serves 8

Roasted Potatoes with Fresh Tomato and Avocado Salsa

FRESH TOMATO AND AVOCADO SALSA
8 to 10 medium plum tomatoes, seeded and
   finely chopped (about 3 cups)
1 cup chopped green onions
3 garlic cloves, minced
1/4 cup olive oil
1 tablespoon lemon juice
salt and pepper to taste
2 medium avocados, peeled and coarsely chopped
   (about 2 cups)

ROASTED POTATOES
4 pounds new potatoes
1/2 cup olive oil
1 tablespoon coarse salt
1 tablespoon chopped fresh rosemary
sour cream (optional)

For the salsa, combine the tomatoes, green onions, garlic, olive oil and lemon juice in a large bowl and mix well. Season with salt and pepper. Add the avocados and mix gently.

For the potatoes, cut the potatoes into halves. Combine with the olive oil, rosemary and salt in a large bowl and toss to coat well. Place cut side down in a lightly oiled shallow roasting pan. Roast at 400 degrees for 20 to 25 minutes or until golden brown, stirring occasionally to prevent sticking.

Remove the potatoes to a large serving platter. Top with the salsa and sour cream.

Serves 12 to 15

Peaches in Wine

12 ripe peaches
4 cups (32 ounces or 1 liter) fruity
   red or white wine
1 cup sugar

Immerse the peaches in boiling water in a saucepan for 5 seconds to loosen the skin. Remove the peaches with a slotted spoon and cool slightly. Remove the skins and slice the peaches, discarding the pits.

Combine the wine and sugar in a glass bowl or punch bowl and stir to dissolve the sugar completely. Add the peaches and mix gently. Chill for 1 hour. Spoon into stemmed glasses to serve.

Serves 16

Orange Tiramisu

1 (10-ounce) pound cake
1 cup orange juice
1 small package vanilla instant pudding mix
2 cups milk
1 cup whipping cream, whipped
2 teaspoons grated orange zest
1 teaspoon orange extract
2 tablespoons baking cocoa

Cut the pound cake crosswise into 1/2-inch slices. Brush both cut sides with the orange juice. Combine the pudding mix and milk in a bowl and whisk for 1 minute or until thick. Fold in the whipped cream, orange zest and orange extract. Spread a thin layer of the pudding mixture in a shallow 2-quart serving dish.

Layer the pound cake and remaining pudding 1/2 at a time in the prepared dish. Sift the baking cocoa over the top. Chill for 3 hours. Garnish with chocolate curls and orange sections.

Serves 12

Feast from the Lodge

Getting their first hunting rifle is a rite of passage for many young Southern men. Our landscape boasts acres of unclaimed forest filled with deer, quail and the occasional hunting lodge. Many of these permanent camps have been in the same family for over a century and were built not only for sport but also for relaxation and reflection. Celebrating the hunt with an elegant feast prepared and served by the hunters is a tradition in many parts of the South. This is how it is done!

Stilton Cheese Spread with Sliced Pears
Oyster and Sausage Bundles
Squash Casserole with Wild Game Sausage
Beer-Glazed Onions
Roasted Vegetables with Fresh Sage
Venison Tenderloin with Blackberries
Rice with Mushrooms
White Chocolate Brandy Alexander
Crème Brûlée
Dessert Coffees

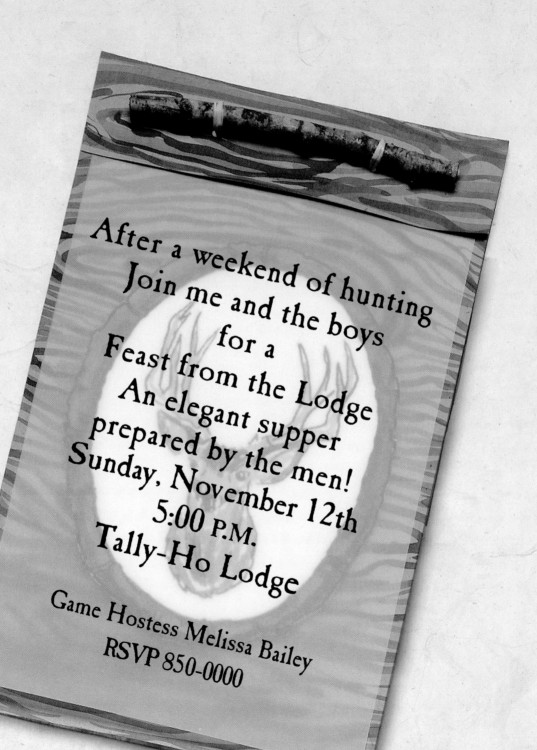

After a weekend of hunting
Join me and the boys
for a
Feast from the Lodge
An elegant supper
prepared by the men!
Sunday, November 12th
5:00 P.M.
Tally-Ho Lodge

Game Hostess Melissa Bailey
RSVP 850-0000

Stilton Cheese Spread with Sliced Pears

12 ounces cream cheese, softened and cubed
1/2 cup (1 stick) unsalted butter, softened, chopped
8 ounces Stilton cheese
1/2 cup chopped toasted walnuts
2 pears, peeled and thinly sliced

Combine the cream cheese and butter in a food processor and pulse until smooth. Crumble the Stilton cheese into the food processor and pulse to mix well. Press the mixture into a 7-inch springform pan lined with plastic wrap. Chill, covered, for 3 hours or until firm.

Remove the side of the springform pan and invert the cheese mixture onto a plate; remove the bottom of the pan and plastic wrap. Invert again onto a serving plate and let stand at room temperature for 1 hour; smooth any cracks in the surface with a wet knife. Sprinkle with the walnuts and arrange the pears around the cheese. Serve with crackers.

Stilton is a blue-veined cheese made from cow's milk and named for the English village where it was first sold. Strong in flavor, it is known as the king of English cheeses.

Serves 12 to 16

Oyster and Sausage Bundles

8 ounces Italian sausage
1/3 cup minced onion
10 ounces fresh oysters, drained
1/2 cup (2 ounces) shredded mozzarella cheese
1/4 cup (1 ounce) shredded sharp Cheddar cheese
1 (17-ounce) package frozen puff pastry sheets, thawed

Remove the sausage from the casings and brown with the onion in a large skillet, stirring until the sausage is crumbly; drain the sausage and skillet and return the sausage to the skillet.

Add the oysters and mix gently. Cook over medium heat for 1 to 2 minutes or just until the edges of the oysters curl. Stir in the mozzarella cheese and Cheddar cheese.

Unfold the pastry sheets on a lightly floured surface. Cut each sheet into 8 rectangles and roll each rectangle into a 5×5-inch square. Spoon the sausage mixture into the center of each square and pull up the sides of the pastry to enclose the filling; twist to seal and spread the edges open above the twist. Freeze, covered, for 1 hour to 1 week.

Place the bundles on an ungreased baking sheet. Bake at 400 degrees for 20 to 22 minutes or until golden brown. Serve immediately.

Makes 16

Squash Casserole with Wild Game Sausage

3 yellow squash, sliced
1 pound wild game sausage or bulk pork sausage,
   crumbled or sliced
1 cup chopped red onion
1 egg
1/4 cup milk
1 cup bread crumbs
1/4 cup (1 ounce) grated Parmesan cheese

Cook the squash in water to cover in a saucepan
until tender; drain. Spoon into an 8- or 9-inch
baking dish.

Cook the sausage in a skillet, stirring until crumbly;
drain. Add to the squash. Sauté the onion in a
nonstick skillet until translucent. Add to the squash
and sausage.

Combine the egg and milk in a small bowl and
mix well. Pour over the squash and sausage mixture.
Mix the bread crumbs and Parmesan cheese in a
bowl and sprinkle over the top. Bake at 350 degrees
for 25 minutes.

Serves 8

BEER-GLAZED ONIONS

Slice 4 large onions 1/4 inch thick. Add to
1/4 cup heated olive oil or butter in a skillet
and sprinkle with 1/2 teaspoon salt,
1/2 teaspoon pepper and a pinch of cayenne
pepper. Sauté over low heat for 20 minutes or
until the onions are golden brown. Add 1/4 cup
porter, bock or other full-flavored beer.
Simmer for 3 to 4 minutes longer or until
the onions are glazed. Serve hot.

Pensacola is blessed with bountiful game
and fish populations and the exceptional
weather that allows hunting and
fishing virtually year-round.
Even December has enough warm days for
saltwater fishing, and freshwater fishing is
only deterred when days turn really cold.

The woods provide exceptional opportunities for hunting deer and turkey in season.
Wing shooters enjoy hunting duck, quail and
dove. The time-honored tradition of sharing
the bounty allows even those who don't hunt
to experience the culinary delights of the bay
area's bountiful game.

Roasted Vegetables with Fresh Sage

6 small zucchini
1 large red bell pepper
20 shallots
6 garlic cloves
3 tablespoons olive oil
1/2 cup chopped fresh sage
1/2 teaspoon salt
1/2 teaspoon freshly ground pepper

Cut the zucchini lengthwise into quarters and
cut the quarters crosswise into halves. Cut the bell
pepper into 1/2-inch strips. Arrange the zucchini,
bell pepper, shallots and garlic in a greased shallow
foil-lined roasting pan.

Drizzle the olive oil over the vegetables. Roast at
500 degrees for 25 minutes. Sprinkle with the sage,
salt and pepper.

Serves 6

Venison Tenderloin with Blackberries

2 venison tenderloins
2 tablespoons sugar cane syrup
1 cup zinfandel
hot pepper sauce to taste
1/4 cup chopped garlic
1/4 cup chopped fresh thyme
1/4 cup chopped fresh basil
1/4 cup chopped fresh tarragon
salt and cracked pepper to taste
1/4 cup (1/2 stick) butter
1 cup fresh blackberries
1/4 cup zinfandel
2 (10-ounce) cans beef consommé

Place the tenderloins on a large baking sheet with a 1-inch rim. Pour the syrup and 1 cup wine over the tenderloins and rub in the syrup. Season with pepper sauce, garlic, thyme, basil, tarragon, salt and pepper and rub in the seasonings. Let stand at room temperature for 4 hours, turning occasionally. Cut the tenderloins into 12 equal medallions.

Melt the butter in a large cast-iron skillet. Add the medallions and sauté until golden brown on both sides or to medium-rare; remove to a platter and keep warm.

Add the blackberries and 1/4 cup wine to the skillet and stir to deglaze the bottom of the skillet. Cook until the mixture is reduced by 1/2. Stir in the beef consommé. Cook until the consommé is reduced to 2 cups. Season with salt and pepper. Return the medallions to the sauce. Cook until heated through.

You may thicken the reduced consommé with a light brown roux if desired.

Serves 6

Rice with Mushrooms

3 cups water
1 1/2 cups dried porcini mushrooms
1 medium onion, coarsely chopped
2 garlic cloves, crushed
2 cups uncooked arborio rice or
    other short-grain rice
1 3/4 cups chicken broth
1/4 teaspoon salt
1/4 teaspoon pepper
2 tablespoons margarine
1/4 cup (1 ounce) grated Parmesan cheese

Bring the water to a boil in a small saucepan and remove from the heat. Add the mushrooms and let stand for 15 minutes; do not drain. Spray a large nonstick skillet with nonstick cooking spray. Add the onion, garlic and rice and sauté over medium heat for 3 to 5 minutes or until golden brown.

Reduce the heat and add the chicken broth, mushrooms with soaking liquid, salt and pepper. Cook, covered, for 11 minutes or until the rice is tender. Remove from the heat and let stand for 5 to 7 minutes or until the liquid is absorbed. Stir in the margarine and Parmesan cheese.

You may substitute shiitake mushrooms for the dried porcini mushrooms if preferred.

Serves 8

White Chocolate Brandy Alexander

3¹/2 cups milk
¹/2 teaspoon vanilla extract
¹/8 teaspoon salt
6 ounces white chocolate, finely chopped
¹/3 cup brandy
3 tablespoons white crème de cacao

Combine the milk, vanilla and salt in a medium saucepan and heat just to the simmering point; do not boil. Pour ¹/4 of the hot milk mixture over the white chocolate in a small bowl and whisk until smooth. Stir the chocolate into the remaining hot milk, stirring constantly. Stir in the brandy and crème de cacao. Pour into serving glasses. Garnish servings with whipped cream and shaved white chocolate.

Serves 4

Crème Brûlée

4 egg yolks
1 teaspoon vanilla extract
¹/4 to ¹/2 cup sugar
2 cups heavy cream
8 teaspoons sugar

Beat the egg yolks with the vanilla in a mixing bowl until thick. Combine ¹/4 to ¹/2 cup sugar with the cream in a saucepan and mix well. Cook over medium heat for 4 to 5 minutes or until steam rises, stirring constantly. Stir a small amount of the hot cream into the egg yolks; stir the egg yolks into the hot cream.

Strain the mixture through a fine sieve into four 7-ounce baking ramekins.

DESSERT COFFEES

Combine ¹/2 cup hot brewed coffee with one of the following flavorings and top with a dollop of whipped cream and a sprinkle of cinnamon or nutmeg:
For Café Alexander, add 1 tablespoon crème de cacao and 1 tablespoon brandy.
For Café Benedictine, add 2 tablespoons Benedictine and 2 tablespoons light cream.
For Café Caribe, add 1 tablespoon coffee liqueur and 1 tablespoon rum.
For Café Colombian, add 2 tablespoons coffee liqueur and 1 tablespoon chocolate syrup.
For Café Dublin, add 1 tablespoon Irish whiskey and 2 teaspoons sugar.
For Café Holland, add 2 tablespoons chocolate mint liqueur.
For Café Israel, add 2 tablespoons chocolate syrup and 2 tablespoons orange liqueur.
For Café Noix, add 2 tablespoons amaretto or Frangelico.

Line a 3-inch deep baking pan with a kitchen towel and place the ramekins in the pan; cover loosely with foil. Add enough boiling water to reach halfway up the sides of the ramekins. Bake at 300 degrees for 30 to 35 minutes or until set. Cool to room temperature. Chill for 2 to 3 hours.

Sprinkle 2 teaspoons sugar over the surface of each custard. Heat the sugar with a kitchen torch, moving the flame over the surface in small circles until the sugar melts and browns.

Serves 4

Entertaining with Old Favorites

The South is steeped in time-honored practices and traditions. Our unique culture is the result of the passing down of rituals from several generations. Luckily, some of our favorite entertaining occasions can be hosted just about anywhere! Give one of these a try!

INITIALLY YOURS

GRACIOUS GARDENERS

WELL-SEASONED SUPPER

Christ Church

INITIALLY YOURS

*The bridal tea is a Southern tradition—an opportunity for all of the women,
young and old, who have been a part of the bride's life to celebrate her approaching marriage.
While "The Tea" is usually a large, well-attended affair, a smaller tea gives the bride a chance
to visit with close friends and family. To add a lovely twist to the tea tradition,
ask each guest to bring an engraved or monogrammed gift. Old or new linen, crystal or silver
will become treasures to last a lifetime.*

Egg Salad Sandwiches with Chive Blossoms
Tomato Provençal Sandwiches
Chutney Cheddar Sandwiches
Walnut Bread
Lemon Raspberry Scones
Apricot Puff Pastry Squares
Gourmet Pecans
Chocolate-Dipped Orange Peel
Victorian Lace Cookies
Peach Pound Cake
Fruit and Mint Iced Tea
Champagne Punch

Bridal Shower Tea
honoring
Christy Moody
August 12th
4:00 P.M.
24 Garden Square
Please bring a gift with the
bride's new initials
C B M

Egg Salad Sandwiches with Chive Blossoms

6 hard-cooked eggs, chopped
2 or 3 tablespoons mayonnaise
1 tablespoon sour cream
1/4 cup chopped seeded peeled cucumber
2 tablespoons chopped salad burnet
2 tablespoons chopped chives
salt and pepper to taste
12 thin slices white bread
unsalted butter, softened
chive blossoms

Combine the hard-cooked eggs, mayonnaise and sour cream in a bowl and mix well. Fold in the cucumber, salad burnet and chives. Season with salt and pepper.

Spread the bread lightly with butter and place on a work surface. Cut into flower shapes with a flower cookie cutter. Spread with the egg mixture. Arrange chive blossoms in a circle in the center of each sandwich to resemble a flower.

You may substitute 1 additional tablespoon chopped chives for the salad burnet if preferred.

Makes 12

The fourth Earl of Sandwich invented the sandwich to meet the requirement of a food easy to eat at the gaming table. Tea sandwiches are models of invention, adapted for the gentle ritual of the tea. Treat each sandwich as a work of art, using cookie cutters for shapes and adding such decorations as edible blossoms and sun-dried tomatoes. For an added touch, moisten the edge of a sandwich and dip it in finely minced parsley.

Tomato Provençal Sandwiches

1 tablespoon chopped basil
1 tablespoon chopped marjoram
1 tablespoon chopped oregano
1 tablespoon chopped thyme
24 thin slices white bread
12 slices small ripe tomatoes
mayonnaise
salt and pepper to taste

Mix the basil, marjoram, oregano and thyme in a small bowl. Cut each slice of bread into a circle the size of the tomato slices. Spread 1 side of each slice with mayonnaise.

Place 1 tomato slice on the spread side of 12 bread circles. Sprinkle with the herb mixture, salt and pepper. Top with the remaining bread circles. Garnish with edible herb blossoms.

Makes 12

Chutney Cheddar Sandwiches

8 ounces smoked chicken or turkey, chopped
4 ounces cream cheese, softened
1 cup (4 ounces) shredded Cheddar cheese
2 tablespoons chutney
1 teaspoon Dijon mustard
1 scallion, thinly sliced
12 slices Walnut Bread (at right), or
    whole wheat bread
unsalted butter, softened
chopped parsley

Combine the chicken, cream cheese, Cheddar cheese, chutney, Dijon mustard and scallion in a mixing bowl and beat at medium speed to mix well.

Trim the crusts from the bread slices. Spread the chicken mixture over 6 slices of the bread and top with the remaining bread slices. Cut each sandwich into 3 fingers.

Spread 1 end of each sandwich finger with butter and press into chopped parsley. Arrange on a serving tray and cover with damp paper towels and plastic wrap until serving time.

Makes 18

Walnut Bread

2 tablespoons honey
1 cup warm (110-degree) water
1 envelope dry yeast
$1^{1}/_{2}$ tablespoons walnut oil
1 teaspoon salt
$1^{1}/_{2}$ cups whole wheat flour
1 cup ground walnuts
$1^{1}/_{2}$ cups (about) all-purpose flour
1 egg
1 tablespoon water

Combine the honey with 1 cup warm water in a large bowl and stir to mix well. Sprinkle the yeast over the surface and let stand for 15 minutes or until dissolved. Add the walnut oil and salt and mix well. Stir in the whole wheat flour, walnuts and enough all-purpose flour gradually to make a soft dough.

Knead on a floured surface for 8 minutes or until smooth and elastic. Place in a buttered bowl, turning to coat the top. Let rise, covered, in a warm place for $1^{1}/_{4}$ to $1^{1}/_{2}$ hours or until doubled in bulk. Punch down the dough and shape into a loaf.

Place in a buttered 5×9-inch loaf pan. Let rise, covered, for 30 to 45 minutes or until doubled in bulk. Whisk the egg with 1 tablespoon water in a small bowl. Brush over the loaf.

Bake at 350 degrees for 35 to 45 minutes or until the loaf sounds hollow when tapped. Remove to a wire rack to cool.

Makes 1 loaf

Lemon Raspberry Scones

2 cups all-purpose flour
1/4 cup sugar
2 1/2 teaspoons baking powder
1/8 teaspoon nutmeg
1/4 teaspoon salt
1/2 cup (1 stick) butter, chilled and chopped
1/2 cup milk
1 egg
1 teaspoon grated lemon zest
3/4 cup fresh raspberries or blueberries
1 tablespoon butter, melted
1 tablespoon sugar

Combine the flour, 1/4 cup sugar, baking powder, nutmeg and salt in a large bowl. Cut in 1/2 cup butter with a pastry blender or 2 knives until the mixture resembles coarse crumbs. Combine the milk, egg and lemon zest in a small bowl and mix well. Add to the dry ingredients and mix with a fork just until moistened and the mixture forms a soft dough. Mix in the raspberries gently.

Shape into a ball and knead on a lightly floured surface 8 to 10 times. Shape into a 9-inch circle 1/2 inch thick on a lightly buttered baking sheet. Cut into 8 wedges with a sharp knife; do not separate. Brush the tops with 1 tablespoon melted butter and sprinkle with 1 tablespoon sugar.

Bake at 425 degrees for 20 to 22 minutes or until golden brown. Cut through the wedges to separate. Serve warm.

Makes 8

No matter where they may appear, monograms tell a story about an individual or even the history of a family. By placing monograms on treasured family items, we show our faith in the future as well as giving a nod to our past. Monograms can adorn linens, silver serving pieces, flatware, china, samplers, pillows, box lids and even jewelry.

Apricot Puff Pastry Squares

1 sheet frozen puff pastry, thawed
1 (16-ounce) can whole apricots in heavy syrup, drained
2 tablespoons honey
4 teaspoons coarse sugar

Unfold the puff pastry sheet and cut into thirds along the creases. Cut the pieces into quarters to make 12 pieces. Arrange on a greased baking sheet.

Cut the apricots into halves, discarding the pits; pat dry. Place 1 apricot cut side down in the center of each pastry. Drizzle with the honey.

Bake at 400 degrees for 12 minutes or until the pastry is puffed around the apricots and golden brown. Sprinkle with the sugar while warm. Cool on a wire rack.

Select the firmest apricots in the can for the best results.

Makes 12

Gourmet Pecans

1 cup packed brown sugar
1¹/2 teaspoons salt
2 large egg whites
¹/4 cup Grand Marnier, Kahlúa or other
   strong-flavored liqueur
4 cups small pecan halves

Mix the brown sugar and salt in a small bowl. Whisk the egg whites and liqueur in a large bowl. Add the pecans, stirring to coat well. Add the brown sugar mixture and mix well. Spread in a single layer in a shallow baking pan lined with foil.

Bake at 325 degrees for 20 to 25 minutes or just until the pecans are toasted and crisp, stirring from the outer edges of the pan toward the center every 10 minutes. Remove the pecans immediately to a waxed paper-lined tray to cool.

Reserve any sugar coating that comes off during the baking process to use as an ice cream topping.

Makes 4 cups

Chocolate-Dipped Orange Peel

3 large thick-skinned oranges
2 cups sugar
2 cups water
4 ounces semisweet chocolate chips

Bring a large saucepan of water to a boil. Cut a slice from the top and bottom of each orange. Cut the peel lengthwise into ¹/2-inch strips and remove from the orange. Cut the strips into ¹/4-inch strips.

Combine the strips with 4 cups of the boiling water in a medium saucepan. Return to a boil and boil for 30 seconds. Drain and rinse under cold water. Repeat the process 3 times adding fresh boiling water each time.

Combine the sugar with 2 cups water in a medium saucepan and bring to a boil. Add the orange strips. Return to a boil and reduce the heat. Simmer for 1 hour or until the strips are tender. Drain and cool for 10 minutes. Remove to a wire rack to cool completely.

Melt the chocolate chips in a double boiler over hot water. Dip ¹/2 to ²/3 of each strip into the chocolate, allowing the excess to drip back into the pan. Place on a waxed paper-lined tray and let stand until the chocolate sets. Store in an airtight container.

Makes 70 to 80

Victorian Lace Cookies

1/2 cup whole wheat flour
1/2 cup rolled oats
1/4 teaspoon baking powder
1/2 cup packed dark brown sugar
1/2 cup chopped pecans
1/4 cup (1/2 stick) butter, melted
2 tablespoons light corn syrup
1/2 teaspoon vanilla extract

Mix the whole wheat flour, oats, baking powder, brown sugar and pecans in a large bowl. Stir in the melted butter, corn syrup and vanilla. Drop by teaspoonfuls 2 inches apart onto a cookie sheet lined with waxed paper.

Bake at 325 degrees for 8 to 10 minutes or until light brown. Cool just enough to handle and remove from the cookie sheet; drape over a lightly buttered rolling pin to curl the cookies. Let stand until cool. Store in an airtight container.

Bake just 1 cookie sheet of cookies at a time and reline the cookie sheet with waxed paper for each batch of cookies.

Makes 3 dozen

Peach Pound Cake

3 cups all-purpose flour
1/4 teaspoon baking soda
1/4 teaspoon salt
2 cups chopped drained fresh peaches
1/2 cup sour cream
1 cup (2 sticks) butter, softened
3 cups sugar
6 eggs
1 teaspoon vanilla extract
1 teaspoon almond extract

Mix the flour, baking soda and salt together. Mix the peaches and sour cream in a bowl.

Cream the butter and sugar in a mixing bowl until light and fluffy. Beat in the eggs 1 at a time. Add the dry ingredients alternately with the peach mixture, mixing well after each addition. Stir in the vanilla and almond extract.

Spoon into a greased and floured bundt pan. Bake at 350 degrees for 1 1/4 hours or until the cake tests done. Cool in the pan for 10 minutes. Remove to a wire rack to cool completely. Garnish with confectioners' sugar and serve with additional peaches and whipped cream.

You may substitute thawed frozen peaches for fresh peaches when they are not in season.

Serves 16

Fruit and Mint Iced Tea

8 to 10 regular tea bags
1/2 cup fresh mint leaves
1 quart boiling water
1 cup sugar
1 (6-ounce) can frozen lemonade concentrate, thawed
1 (6-ounce) can frozen limeade concentrate, thawed
3/4 cup orange juice
3 quarts cold water

Combine the tea bags and mint leaves with the boiling water in a pitcher. Steep, covered for 30 minutes; discard the tea bags. Add the sugar, lemonade concentrate, limeade concentrate and orange juice, stirring until the sugar dissolves.

Strain into a 1 1/2-gallon container and add 3 quarts cold water. Chill until serving time. Garnish servings with additional fresh mint leaves.

Makes 4 1/2 quarts

Tea strainers or petits fours marked with the honoree's monogram and wrapped in boxes to go make nice favors for an Initially Yours party. It's a good opportunity for the hostess to bring out all of her treasured monogrammed silver, china and linens.

Champagne Punch

1 quart water
1 family-size tea bag
2 cups sugar
2 cups lemon juice
2 cups lime juice
1 quart club soda, chilled
3 (25-ounce) bottles Champagne, chilled

Bring the water to a boil in a large saucepan and add the tea bag. Steep, covered, for 3 to 4 minutes; discard the tea bag. Add the sugar, lemon juice and lime juice, stirring until the sugar dissolves. Chill until serving time.

Combine with the club soda and Champagne in a punch bowl at serving time and mix gently.

Makes 5 1/2 quarts

GRACIOUS GARDENERS

*Gardening provides a human connection that is particularly attractive to Southerners.
A casual walk through most any backyard includes living reminders—Grandmother's hydrangea,
Uncle Frank's dogwood, Mama's daylilies—of gifts from the gardens of others. Throw a luncheon
for your gardening friends and encourage everyone to bring a plant or cutting to exchange.
Remember, though, gardening lore promises bad luck for your new transplant if you say, "Thank you!"*

CHÈVRE TWISTS

CHILLED AVOCADO SOUP

STRAWBERRY AND FETA SALAD

CHICKEN BREASTS FILLED WITH SPINACH AND RICOTTA

BAKED TOMATOES WITH GARLIC AND BASIL

OVEN-ROASTED ASPARAGUS WITH HAZELNUT VINAIGRETTE

PEACH AND BLUEBERRY COBBLER WITH STRAWBERRY CRÈME FRAÎCHE

LIME AND HONEYDEW SORBET CUPS

DAISY COOKIES

Join Me for a
GARDENERS' LUNCHEON
Friday, April 16th
12:00 noon
THE BARKLEY HOUSE
Please bring your favorite potted plant
complete with planting and growing instructions!
Brantlee Vinson

*M*ost fresh herbs will keep for up to a week in the refrigerator. Herbs with tender stems, such as parsley, should be placed in a glass of water and covered with a plastic bag. Herbs with woody stems, such as thyme and rosemary, should be sealed in a plastic bag. For longer storage, tender-stemmed herbs can be puréed and frozen in oil or water, using about 1/2 cup liquid for each two cups of herbs.

Chèvre Twists

4 ounces chèvre
1 cup pitted kalamata olives
1 tablespoon fresh rosemary
2 tablespoons chopped fresh basil
1 sheet frozen puff pastry, thawed

*C*ombine the chèvre, olives, rosemary and basil in a food processor and process until smooth.

Unfold the puff pastry sheet and place on a lightly floured surface; roll into a 10×12-inch rectangle. Spread the cheese mixture lengthwise over half the pastry, spreading to within 1 inch of the long edge; fold the remaining pastry over the cheese mixture. Roll lightly to press and pinch the edges to seal.

Cut crosswise into twenty 1/2-inch strips. Twist each strip 3 times and arrange on a lightly greased baking sheet. Bake at 400 degrees for 12 to 15 minutes or until golden brown. Remove to a wire rack to cool. Store in an airtight container.

Makes 20

Chilled Avocado Soup

2 large ripe avocados
lemon juice
2 cups chicken broth
3 tablespoons fresh lemon juice
1 cup buttermilk
1/2 teaspoon curry powder
salt to taste
1 cup plain yogurt or sour cream

*C*hop 11/2 of the avocados; sprinkle the remaining avocado half with lemon juice and reserve. Combine the chopped avocado with the chicken broth and 3 tablespoons lemon juice in a food processor or blender and process until smooth. Add the buttermilk, curry powder and salt and process to mix well. Remove to a bowl and chill in the refrigerator for 2 hours or longer.

Cut the reserved avocado into thin slices. Top servings of the soup with the sliced avocado and a dollop of the yogurt.

Serves 6

STRAWBERRY AND FETA SALAD

*H*eat 1/2 cup sugar with 1/2 cup white vinegar in a small saucepan, stirring until the sugar dissolves. Add 1/2 cup vegetable oil, 2 teaspoons minced garlic, 1/2 teaspoon dry mustard, 1/2 teaspoon paprika and 1/2 teaspoon salt and mix well. Cool and chill until serving time. Serve over a salad of baby lettuce and quartered strawberries and sprinkle with feta cheese.

Chicken Breasts Filled with Spinach and Ricotta

1 cup ricotta cheese or low-fat ricotta cheese
1/4 cup (1 ounce) grated Parmesan cheese
1 cup chopped fresh spinach
3 scallions with a portion of the green tops, chopped
1/4 cup sliced fresh basil
1/4 cup chopped fresh parsley
1/2 teaspoon dried thyme
1/4 teaspoon nutmeg
3/4 teaspoon salt
1/4 teaspoon pepper
6 boneless chicken breasts with skin
1 tablespoon olive oil
salt and pepper to taste

Combine the ricotta cheese, Parmesan cheese, spinach, scallions, basil, parsley, thyme, nutmeg, 3/4 teaspoon salt and 1/4 teaspoon pepper in a bowl and mix well. Loosen the skin from the chicken breasts, but do not remove. Place 2 tablespoons of the spinach mixture under the loosened skin and press the skin back in place, tucking the ends under.

Arrange the chicken in a baking dish. Drizzle with the olive oil and sprinkle with additional salt and pepper to taste. Bake at 350 degrees for 35 minutes.

Cool the chicken to room temperature. Slice crosswise and arrange on a lettuce-lined serving platter. Garnish with fresh basil leaves.

Serves 6

Governor George Johnstone was dispatched to Pensacola in 1764 and found a handful of hovels peopled by Spaniards who seemed to have priorities other than producing food. He put in place a new plan to make the colony more self-sufficient. He established well-mapped residential plots on the southern edge of the town and a series of garden plots to the north, where he expected the residents to produce a variety of produce. A person who acquired a home site also received a garden plot. This area is now known as Garden Street.

Baked Tomatoes with Garlic and Basil

6 medium firm tomatoes
10 basil leaves
salt to taste
extra-virgin olive oil
6 garlic cloves, chopped

Core the tomatoes and arrange snugly in a baking dish with cored ends down. Insert 10 basil leaves between the tomatoes and sprinkle with salt. Add enough olive oil to reach 1/4 of the way up the sides of the tomatoes; immerse the basil leaves into the olive oil to prevent burning. Sprinkle with garlic.

Bake at 350 degrees for 1 to 1 1/4 hours or until the tomatoes are very tender and begin to brown on top. Remove the tomatoes to a serving dish and spoon a small amount of the oil over the tops. Garnish with additional fresh basil.

Serves 6

Bring 1 cup sugar and 1 cup water to a boil in a small saucepan. Add the peels of 2 lemons and simmer for 2 minutes. Let stand for 45 minutes or until cool. Crush 1 cup mint leaves in a medium bowl and pour the sugar syrup over the leaves. Let stand for 1 to 2 hours. Strain into a bowl and add the juice of 2 lemons. Fill 8 to 10 chilled small glasses or mint julep cups with finely crushed ice and add 2 tablespoons of the syrup and 3 tablespoons bourbon to each glass. Mix gently and garnish with mint sprigs. Serve immediately.

Oven-Roasted Asparagus with Hazelnut Vinaigrette

2 tablespoons finely chopped hazelnuts
2 tablespoons minced shallots
1 tablespoon hazelnut oil
1 tablespoon red wine vinegar
1/2 teaspoon Dijon mustard
1 pound fresh asparagus
1 tablespoon olive oil
1/4 teaspoon each salt and pepper

Combine the hazelnuts, shallots, hazelnut oil, vinegar and Dijon mustard in a small bowl and whisk until smooth.

Arrange the asparagus on a baking sheet; drizzle with olive oil; sprinkle with salt and pepper. Roast at 500 degrees for 8 minutes, turning once. Remove to a serving platter and drizzle with the vinaigrette.

Serves 6

Peach and Blueberry Cobbler with Strawberry Crème Fraîche

STRAWBERRY CRÈME FRAÎCHE
1/2 cup buttermilk
1/2 cup heavy cream
4 strawberries, mashed
1 teaspoon vanilla extract

COBBLER
1 1/2 cups packed light brown sugar
6 tablespoons all-purpose flour
juice of 3 lemons
1 teaspoon cinnamon
1 teaspoon nutmeg
1 tablespoon vanilla extract
6 fresh peaches, peeled, sliced
1 1/2 cups fresh blueberries

For the crème fraîche, whisk the buttermilk and heavy cream together in a bowl. Let stand at room temperature for 1 hour or longer. Add the strawberries and vanilla and mix well.

For the cobbler, combine the brown sugar, flour, lemon juice, cinnamon, nutmeg and vanilla in a bowl and mix well. Add the peaches and blueberries and mix gently.

Spoon the fruit mixture into a baking dish. Bake at 350 degrees until the fruit is tender and the top is golden brown. Serve with the crème fraîche spooned over the top.

Serves 6

Lime and Honeydew Sorbet Cups

LIME SORBET AND SORBET CUPS
6 large limes
2 teaspoons grated lime zest
3/4 cup sugar
1 tablespoon vodka

HONEYDEW SORBET
1 honeydew melon
1 cup sugar
1 tablespoon lime juice
1 tablespoon vodka

For the lime sorbet and cups, cut off the top third of each lime. Squeeze the juice into a cup and reserve the juice and the rinds. Cut and scoop out the remaining membranes from the limes to make the cups. Cut a thin slice from the bottom of the cups to help them stand evenly. Place the cups and tops into airtight sealable plastic bags and freeze until serving time.

Measure 1/2 cup lime juice and strain the juice into a large bowl. Add the lime zest, sugar and vodka and mix until the sugar dissolves. Chill in the refrigerator.

Pour the lime mixture into an ice cream freezer container and freeze until firm using the manufacturer's instructions. Remove to a freezer container and place a piece of plastic wrap directly on the surface. Freeze for up to 3 days.

For the honeydew sorbet, cut the honeydew melon into halves and scoop the flesh into a food processor. Process until puréed. Measure 2 cups purée, adding water if necessary for the amount.

Combine the honeydew purée, sugar, lime juice and vodka in a large bowl and mix until the sugar dissolves. Chill in the refrigerator.

Pour the honeydew mixture into an ice cream freezer container and freeze until firm using the manufacturer's instructions. Remove to a freezer container and place a piece of plastic wrap directly on the surface. Freeze for up to 3 days.

To serve, place 1 lime cup in each of 6 serving bowls. Place 1 scoop of lime sorbet and 1 scoop of honeydew sorbet in each cup. Garnish each with a sprig of mint and place the lime tops at an angle on the sorbet. Serve immediately.

Serves 6

Daisy Cookies

2 1/2 cups all-purpose flour, sifted
1/2 teaspoon salt
1 cup (2 sticks) unsalted butter, softened
2/3 cup sugar
1 egg
3/4 teaspoon almond extract

Mix the flour and salt together. Cream the butter and sugar in a mixing bowl until light and fluffy. Add the egg and almond extract and mix well. Add the flour mixture and mix well. Divide into 3 portions and wrap each portion in plastic wrap. Chill for 2 to 8 hours.

Roll 1 portion of the dough at a time 1/4 inch thick on a lightly floured surface. Cut with a scalloped cookie cutter and arrange on a cookie sheet. Bake at 350 degrees for 8 to 10 minutes or until golden brown. Cool on the cookie sheet for several minutes. Remove to a wire rack to cool completely.

You may frost the cookies with white frosting and pipe yellow frosting into the centers or sprinkle sugar colored with yellow food coloring into the centers if desired.

Makes 2 dozen

WELL-SEASONED SUPPER

*Summer is the time of year we enjoy the fresh produce that the sun
has coaxed from our well-tended gardens. If you haven't discovered
the joy of growing your own vegetables, the local farmers' market
can provide! Picture a colorful spread of tomatoes, beans, asparagus,
and peppers—all freshly prepared and perfectly seasoned.
Now invite a group of friends for good food and good company.
Enjoyed earlier in the evening,
Southerners call this traditional meal "supper."*

FRESH ASPARAGUS WITH TOMATOES
CARAMELIZED VIDALIA ONION DIP
BLACK-EYED PEA CORN MUFFINS WITH PIMENTO CHEESE
GAZPACHO WITH CRAB MEAT
ROASTED CHICKEN
GREEN BEANS WITH TOASTED PINE NUT OIL
COLLARD GREENS
BOURBON BANANA PUDDING
STRAWBERRY AND WATERMELON LEMONADE
ICED TEA SOUTHERN STYLE

Celebrate Summer's Bountiful Harvest
With a Well-Seasoned Supper
Please join us
Saturday, August 5th At 6:30 P.M.
2525 Sunset Road

Lisa & Mark Greskovich

RSVP 850-1265

Fresh Asparagus with Tomatoes

2 pounds fresh asparagus
6 medium tomatoes, thinly sliced
1/3 cup shredded mozzarella cheese
2 to 3 tablespoons chopped fresh basil
3 to 4 tablespoons balsamic vinegar

Snap off the tough ends of the asparagus. Combine with a small amount of boiling water in a saucepan and cook for 4 to 6 minutes or just until tender-crisp. Drain the asparagus and plunge into ice water to stop the cooking process; drain.

Arrange the tomato slices around the outer edge of a large serving platter. Sprinkle with the cheese and basil; drizzle with the balsamic vinegar. Arrange the asparagus in the center.

Serves 12

Caramelized Vidalia Onion Dip

2 tablespoons butter
2 tablespoons vegetable oil
2 large Vidalia onions, cut into quarters and thinly sliced
1/4 cup chopped red bell pepper
1/4 cup chopped yellow bell pepper
1/4 cup chopped garlic
1 cup sour cream
1 cup mayonnaise
1/4 cup sliced green onions
1 tablespoon chopped parsley
1 tablespoon chopped purple basil
1 tablespoon chopped thyme
hot pepper sauce to taste
salt and cracked pepper to taste

Heat the butter and vegetable oil in a heavy sauté pan over medium-high heat. Add the onions and sauté for 30 to 45 minutes or until caramelized and golden brown, stirring constantly. Add the bell peppers and garlic and sauté for 3 to 5 minutes longer. Spoon into a large bowl and let stand until cool.

Add the sour cream, mayonnaise, green onions, parsley, basil and thyme and mix well. Season with hot sauce, salt and pepper. Spoon into a serving bowl and place on a platter with garlic croutons, crackers or chips for dipping.

Serves 10 to 12

Serve tomatoes at room temperature. Slice them, arrange them on a platter, add a few fresh basil leaves from the garden, and drizzle with balsamic vinegar or homemade mayonnaise.

Black-Eyed Pea Corn Muffins with Pimento Cheese

PIMENTO CHEESE
2¹/2 cups (10 ounces) shredded sharp Cheddar
    cheese
1 (4-ounce) jar sliced pimentos
grated onion to taste
2 teaspoons finely minced jalapeño pepper
Worcestershire sauce to taste
¹/2 to 1 cup mayonnaise

BLACK-EYED PEA CORN MUFFINS
1 onion, chopped
¹/2 cup chopped green bell pepper
3 (7-ounce) packages corn bread mix
³/4 cup cream-style corn
2 cups (8 ounces) shredded Cheddar cheese
1 (15-ounce) can black-eyed peas, drained
Tabasco sauce to taste

For the pimento cheese, combine the Cheddar cheese, undrained pimentos, onion, jalapeño pepper and Worcestershire sauce in a microwave-safe bowl. Microwave just until the cheese is softened; mix well. Cool to room temperature and mix in enough mayonnaise to make of the desired consistency.

For the muffins, sauté the onion and bell pepper in a nonstick skillet until tender.

Prepare the corn bread mixes using the package directions. Add the onion and pepper mixture, corn, cheese, peas and Tabasco sauce; mix well.

Spoon into greased muffin cups. Bake at 350 degrees for 25 to 30 minutes or until golden brown. Serve with the pimento cheese.

You may add browned bulk hot pork sausage, jalapeño peppers and/or use Mexican corn bread mix for a zestier version of the corn muffins.

Serves 12

Gazpacho with Crab Meat

3 pounds ripe tomatoes, seeded and coarsely
    chopped (about 6 cups)
1 cup coarsely chopped yellow onion
1 red or yellow bell pepper, seeded and coarsely
    chopped
1 tablespoon coarsely chopped garlic
1 teaspoon chopped serrano pepper
6 tablespoons coarsely chopped cilantro
¹/4 cup olive oil
2 tablespoons red wine vinegar
¹/4 teaspoon sugar
¹/4 cup fresh lime juice
1¹/2 cups (or less) tomato juice
1 cup chopped fresh fennel
salt to taste
1 (6-ounce) can crab meat, drained
1 teaspoon lime juice
pepper to taste

Combine the tomatoes, onion, bell pepper, garlic, serrano pepper, cilantro, olive oil, vinegar, sugar and ¹/4 cup lime juice in a large bowl. Add to the food processor in 2 batches and pulse until coarsely chopped. Add 1 cup tomato juice and pulse until of the desired consistency, adding the remaining ¹/2 cup tomato juice if desired. Combine the batches in a large bowl and add the fennel and salt to taste. Chill until serving time.

Combine the crab meat with 1 teaspoon lime juice in a small bowl. Season with pepper.

To serve, ladle the gazpacho into bowls or hollowed-out tomatoes. Spoon the crab meat into the centers. Garnish with a sprig of fennel greens.

Serves 6

Roasted Chicken

2 (3- to 3 1/2-pound) chickens
juice of 1 lemon
8 garlic cloves, crushed
1 lemon, cut into quarters
6 sprigs fresh rosemary
1 tablespoon olive oil
salt and pepper to taste
3 or 4 large onions (optional)
olive oil
1 garlic bulb (optional)

*T*uck the wing tips of the chicken under and rub with the lemon juice. Loosen the skin over the breasts with the fingers and place some of the crushed garlic and 1 sprig of rosemary under the skin of each side of the breasts; rub crushed garlic over the skin. Place the remaining crushed garlic, 2 lemon quarters and 1 rosemary sprig in the cavity of each chicken. Rub the chickens with 1 tablespoon olive oil and sprinkle with salt and pepper. Place the chickens on their sides on a rack in a roasting pan or directly in the roasting pan.

Cut the onions into halves and rub with additional olive oil. Remove the papery skin from the garlic bulb and rub with a small amount of additional olive oil. Place the onions and garlic bulb in the roasting pan. Let stand for 15 minutes.

Place a meat thermometer in the thickest inside portion of the thigh of one chicken; do not allow to touch the bone. Roast at 425 degrees for 15 minutes. Turn the chickens breast side up and roast for 15 minutes longer. Reduce the oven temperature to 350 degrees. Pour 1 cup of water into the roasting pan if necessary to reduce spattering.

Roast at 350 degrees for 30 to 40 minutes longer to 180 degrees on the meat thermometer or until the juices run clear when the thigh is pierced with a knife. Serve with roasted vegetables and polenta.

GREEN BEANS WITH TOASTED PINE NUT OIL

*C*ombine 3 pounds tender-crisp green beans and 6 tablespoons olive oil mixed with 1 cup toasted pine nuts, coarsely ground, in a bowl. Toss gently and season with salt to taste.

You may serve 1 chicken for dinner and pull the meat from the remaining chicken and chill, loosely covered. Place the chilled chicken in a sealable plastic bag for later use.

Serves 8 to 10

Collard Greens

1 large bunch collard greens
3 cups water
chopped ham or sausage
Worcestershire sauce to taste
salt and pepper to taste
sugar or honey to taste (optional)
vinegar to taste (optional)

*W*ash the greens well, discarding the stems. Chop the greens into bite-size pieces. Pour the water into a 5-quart saucepan. Alternate layers of the greens and ham in the saucepan, sprinkling the layers with Worcestershire sauce, salt and pepper.

Bring to a boil and boil for 10 minutes. Reduce the heat to medium and cook for 30 minutes. Add sugar or vinegar as needed for taste. Cook for 15 minutes longer or until tender, depending on the tenderness of the greens. Serve with hot sauce.

Serves 4

Bourbon Banana Pudding

1 1/4 cups sugar
3/4 cup all-purpose flour
4 cups milk
8 large egg yolks, beaten
1/2 teaspoon salt
2 teaspoons vanilla extract
2 tablespoons rum
2 tablespoons bourbon
2 cups whole vanilla wafers
1 1/2 cups broken toffee or almond roca bars
8 bananas, sliced
2 cups whipping cream
1 tablespoon sugar
1/2 teaspoon vanilla extract

Combine 1 1/4 cups sugar, flour, milk, egg yolks, salt and 2 teaspoons vanilla in a double boiler and mix well. Place over simmering water and cook until the mixture thickens enough to heavily coat the back of a wooden spoon, stirring constantly. Place in an ice water bath and stir for 15 minutes to stop the cooking process.

Mix the rum and bourbon in a cup. Place the vanilla wafers on a work surface and brush with the rum mixture. Reserve 1/2 cup of the candy pieces. Layer the vanilla wafers, cooled custard, bananas and remaining candy pieces 1/2 at a time in a glass dish or trifle bowl.

Combine the whipping cream, 1 tablespoon sugar and 1/2 teaspoon vanilla in a mixing bowl and beat until soft peaks form. Spread over the pudding and sprinkle with the reserved candy pieces. Chill until serving time.

Serves 12

Strawberry and Watermelon Lemonade

1 (6-pound) watermelon
2 pints strawberries, hulled
1/2 cup sugar
1 (12-ounce) can frozen lemonade concentrate, thawed
3/4 cup fresh lemon juice

Cut the watermelon into chunks, discarding the seeds. Purée the watermelon in batches in a food processor. Strain into a large bowl or 2-quart pitcher.

Process the strawberries with the sugar in a food processor until smooth. Add to the watermelon purée with the lemonade concentrate and lemon juice; mix well. Chill until serving time.

Serves 8

ICED TEA SOUTHERN STYLE

It's easy to make southern-style iced tea. For one quart of tea, bring 2 cups of cold water to a boil in a nonaluminum saucepan. Add three tea bags of plain black tea such as orange pekoe and remove from the heat. Steep, covered, for 5 minutes or longer. Remove the tea bags and stir in 1/4 to 1/2 cup sugar, or to taste. Combine with about 2 cups cold water in a pitcher. Serve over ice.

Entertaining from Dawn to Dusk

Plenty of sunny days help simplify party planning in Pensacola, but other activities still compete for the mere twenty-four hours each day brings. When scheduling is a problem, get creative! Plan a party during an unusual time or coordinate a gathering with another event. After all, you have from dawn to dusk!

BREAKFAST OF CHAMPIONS

BOXED LUNCH ON BLACKWATER

STARGAZING AT FORT PICKENS

Waiting for the Belle

BREAKFAST OF CHAMPIONS

*The Santa Rosa Island Triathlon was recently voted "Best Large Triathlon" by readers
of a national magazine. Competitors run, bike and swim their way to the finish line
in the popular event hosted at Pensacola Beach each fall. After months of training,
most of the athletes count finishing the race a reason to celebrate!
Here's a menu that will satisfy the heartiest of appetites. Invite the athletes and their fans
for a breakfast of champions—let the party begin!*

OREGANO CHEESE PUFFS

GINGERED FRUIT SALAD

VEGETABLE FRITTATA

SAUSAGE AND CHEESE MUFFINS

APPLE PECAN WAFFLES

GARLIC CHEESE GRITS SOUFFLÉ

POPPY SEED BREAD WITH ORANGE GLAZE

SMOOTHIE BAR

Oregano Cheese Puffs

3/4 cup milk
3 tablespoons butter
3/4 cup all-purpose flour
1/2 teaspoon salt
1/8 teaspoon pepper
3 large eggs
1/4 cup (1 ounce) shredded fontina cheese
1 1/2 teaspoons dried oregano
1/4 cup (1 ounce) shredded fontina cheese

Bring the milk and butter to a simmer in a medium saucepan and reduce the heat to low. Add the flour, salt and pepper all at once and stir constantly until the mixture leaves the side of the saucepan and forms a smooth ball. Remove from the heat and let stand for 5 to 10 minutes.

Beat in the eggs 1 at a time. Add 1/4 cup cheese and oregano and mix well. Drop by level tablespoonfuls onto a greased baking sheet. Bake at 400 degrees for 18 minutes.

Sprinkle with 1/4 cup cheese and bake for 2 to 3 minutes longer or until the cheese melts. Serve immediately.

Makes 2 1/2 dozen

Decorations for a breakfast of champions could include well-worn—and well washed—running shoes spray-painted with gold or silver and used to hold flowers. Spray paint goggles to use as decorations along with ribbons and medals. Line bicycle helmets with cloth napkins to hold the bread and muffins and add paper products that coordinate with the colors of the race shirts.

Gingered Fruit Salad

3 cups green seedless grape halves
3 cups hulled strawberry halves
3 Granny Smith apples, chopped
1 (11-ounce) can mandarin oranges, drained
8 ounces cream cheese, softened
1/3 cup orange juice
2 tablespoons sugar
1/2 teaspoon ground ginger

Combine the grapes, strawberries, apples and oranges in a large bowl. Combine the cream cheese, orange juice, sugar and ginger in a small bowl and mix until smooth. Add to the fruit and toss gently. Serve immediately.

Serves 8

Vegetable Frittata

1/2 cup (1 stick) butter
2 bunches scallions, sliced
12 ounces shiitake mushrooms, sliced
1 (10-ounce) package frozen chopped spinach,
    thawed
2 cups chopped artichoke hearts
4 small unpeeled red potatoes, cooked and
    chopped
2 tablespoons pine nuts, toasted
10 eggs
1 cup half-and-half
1 cup (4 ounces) shredded Monterey Jack cheese
1 cup (4 ounces) shredded sharp Cheddar cheese
salt and pepper to taste

Melt the butter in a skillet and add the scallions, mushrooms, spinach, artichoke hearts, potatoes and pine nuts. Sauté until the vegetables are tender. Spread in a greased 9×13-inch baking dish.

Beat the eggs with the half-and-half in a large bowl. Add the Monterey Jack cheese, Cheddar cheese, salt and pepper and mix well. Pour over the vegetables.

Bake at 350 degrees for 25 minutes or until light brown and done to taste. Serve immediately.

You may top with chopped tomatoes, roasted garlic and/or chopped purple onion if desired.

Serves 10

Sausage and Cheese Muffins

8 ounces bulk pork sausage
1/4 cup chopped green onions
1/4 cup chopped green bell pepper
3/4 cup all-purpose flour
1/2 cup cornmeal
1 teaspoon baking soda
1/2 teaspoon salt
1/8 teaspoon red pepper
1 cup buttermilk
1 egg, beaten
1/2 cup (2 ounces) shredded Cheddar cheese

Brown the sausage with the green onions and bell pepper in a skillet over medium heat, stirring until the sausage is crumbly; drain.

Mix the flour, cornmeal, baking soda, salt and red pepper in a bowl. Blend the buttermilk and egg in a small bowl. Add the buttermilk mixture, sausage mixture and cheese to the flour mixture and stir just until moistened.

Spoon into greased muffin cups, filling 2/3 full. Bake at 400 degrees for 28 to 30 minutes or until golden brown.

Makes 12

The basic theme of the breakfast of champions could be used to celebrate many other sporting events, such as tennis tournaments, runs, golf, baseball, soccer or swim meets. Just use the equipment appropriate to the sport for the decorations.

Apple Pecan Waffles

APPLE PECAN SAUCE
1 tablespoon lemon juice
1 tablespoon dark rum
3/4 cup water
1/4 teaspoon cinnamon
3 Golden Delicious apples, peeled and sliced
1 cup heavy cream
4 1/2 tablespoons dark brown sugar
1 tablespoon unsalted butter
1 tablespoon dark rum
6 tablespoons chopped pecans, toasted

WAFFLES
3 eggs
3/4 cup sugar
5 cups all-purpose flour
1 tablespoon baking powder
1 teaspoon salt
1 quart buttermilk
1/2 cup (1 stick) butter, melted

For the sauce, combine the lemon juice, 1 tablespoon rum, water and cinnamon in a bowl and mix well. Add the apple slices and toss to coat well. Spread in a baking pan. Bake at 375 degrees for 20 minutes.

Combine the heavy cream and brown sugar in a small saucepan and cook for 6 to 8 minutes or until thickened, stirring constantly. Add the butter, 1 tablespoon rum and pecans and cook just until the butter melts. Add to the apple mixture and mix well. Keep warm.

For the waffles, beat the eggs in a mixing bowl for 2 minutes. Add the sugar, flour, baking powder, salt, buttermilk and butter and mix well.

Cook in a waffle iron using the manufacturer's instructions. Serve with the warm apple pecan sauce.

Serves 6

Garlic Cheese Grits Soufflé

4 cups water
1 teaspoon salt
1 cup uncooked grits
1 cup (4 ounces) shredded sharp Cheddar cheese
1/2 cup (1 stick) butter
3 garlic cloves, minced
3 egg whites

Combine the water and salt in a saucepan and bring to a boil. Stir in the grits gradually and reduce the heat. Simmer for 15 minutes, stirring frequently. Remove from the heat and stir in the cheese and butter until melted. Mix in the garlic. Let stand, covered, until cool.

Beat the egg whites in a mixing bowl until stiff peaks form. Fold into the grits mixture. Spoon into a baking dish sprayed with nonstick cooking spray. Bake at 350 degrees for 30 to 40 minutes or until set. Let stand for 5 minutes before serving.

You may prepare the grits ahead of time and fold in the egg whites just before baking.

Serves 8 to 12

Poppy Seed Bread with Orange Glaze

BREAD
3 cups all-purpose flour
2$\frac{1}{4}$ cups sugar
1$\frac{1}{2}$ teaspoons baking powder
1$\frac{1}{2}$ teaspoons salt
1$\frac{1}{2}$ teaspoons poppy seeds
1$\frac{1}{2}$ cups vegetable oil
3 eggs
1$\frac{1}{2}$ cups milk
1$\frac{1}{2}$ teaspoons each butter, almond and vanilla
   flavorings

ORANGE GLAZE
$\frac{3}{4}$ cup confectioners' sugar
$\frac{1}{4}$ cup orange juice
$\frac{1}{2}$ teaspoon each butter, almond and vanilla
   flavorings

For the bread, mix the flour, sugar, baking powder, salt and poppy seeds in a mixing bowl. Add the vegetable oil, eggs, milk and flavorings. Beat for 2 minutes. Spoon into 2 large or 3 medium loaf pans.

Bake at 350 degrees for 1 hour. Cool in the pans for 10 minutes. Remove to a wire rack.

For the glaze, combine the confectioners' sugar, orange juice and flavorings in a bowl and mix well.

Pierce the hot loaves all over with a fork and brush the glaze over the tops. Let stand until cool.

Makes 2 large or 3 medium loaves

Invest in a heavy-duty blender for the smoothie bar. It will ensure smooth and well-blended drinks for the party, and your family will find it a good way to enjoy fruit drinks all year.

Smoothie Bar

1 cup vanilla yogurt
$\frac{1}{2}$ cup fruit juice
$\frac{1}{2}$ cup sliced fruit or whole berries
$\frac{1}{2}$ cup ice cubes

Combine the yogurt, juice, fruit and ice cubes in a blender. Process for 1 minute or until smooth. Pour into a glass to serve.

You may use any 100% fruit juice, such as orange juice, cranberry juice, grapefruit juice or pineapple juice, or a mixture to suit individual tastes. Fresh fruits might include bananas, mangoes, peaches, kiwifruit, blueberries, strawberries or raspberries.

Serves 1

Boxed Lunch on Blackwater

While the Pensacola area is best known for its beaches, the Blackwater River is a refreshing change of scenery that both visitors and locals enjoy. The cool flowing water makes midday a good time for canoeing or tubing, and the plentiful sandbars provide ideal stops for an old-fashioned boxed lunch. In the South, boxed lunches are often packed with fried chicken—a favorite on this side of the Mason-Dixon. Try the famous recipe from Pensacola's Hopkins House, and you'll be hooked, too.

APPETIZER FRUIT CUP
CORA EDWARDS' FRIED CHICKEN
CREOLE POTATO SALAD
MARINATED VEGETABLES
QUICK AND EASY YEAST ROLLS
CARAMEL-FILLED CHOCOLATE COOKIES
PEANUT BUTTER AND CHOCOLATE CHUNK COOKIES
PRALINE COOKIES
ORANGE MINT LEMONADE

Join us for a Moveable Feast

Saturday, July 10th, 10 A.M., Blackwater River

Enjoy the lazy days of summer as we feast and drift downstream.
Tubes and swimsuits encouraged.

Julie and Donald Krehely

850-8000

Appetizer Fruit Cup

1 cup honeydew melon balls
1 cup cantaloupe balls
1 cup strawberry halves
6 tablespoons Cointreau or other orange liqueur

Combine the honeydew melon balls, cantaloupe balls and strawberries in a bowl. Add the liqueur and toss to coat well. Chill, covered, for up to 2 hours. Spoon into serving bowls and garnish with mint leaves.

Serves 2 or 3

Cora Edwards' Fried Chicken

1 chicken
salt to taste
self-rising flour
vegetable oil

Cut up the chicken and sprinkle it generously with salt. Cover and place in the refrigerator for 8 hours or longer. Coat well with the flour.

Heat vegetable oil to 350 degrees in a skillet. Add the chicken and fry for 7 minutes or until golden brown, turning to brown evenly.

This recipe came from the renowned Hopkins House. Cora Edwards' fried chicken was voted "Number 1 Fried Chicken in America" by *USA Today* in 2000.

Serves 5

For a canoeing picnic, pack lunches in white boxes from a bakery or restaurant supply house. Place the boxes in coolers and seal with tape to ensure waterproofing. Place a watermelon in a mesh laundry bag to chill in the cold water by lunchtime.

Creole Potato Salad

3 pounds red potatoes, chopped
salt to taste
1/2 cup mayonnaise
1/2 cup Creole mustard
1 tablespoon red wine vinegar
1 teaspoon prepared horseradish
1/2 teaspoon chopped fresh thyme
1/4 teaspoon garlic powder
1 teaspoon salt
1/4 teaspoon ground red pepper
6 hard-cooked eggs, chopped
1 medium onion, chopped
1/4 cup capers

Cook the potatoes in salted boiling water in a saucepan until tender; drain and cool slightly.

Combine the mayonnaise, Creole mustard, vinegar, horseradish, thyme, garlic powder, salt and red pepper in a bowl and mix well. Add the potatoes, eggs, onion and capers and toss gently. Serve chilled or at room temperature.

Serves 6

Marinated Vegetables

1 1/2 cups vegetable oil
1 cup cider vinegar
1 tablespoon sugar
1 to 3 teaspoons dried dillweed
1 teaspoon garlic salt
1 teaspoon salt
1 teaspoon pepper
florets of 1 pound broccoli
florets of 1 head cauliflower
5 yellow squash, thinly sliced
5 medium carrots, diagonally sliced
6 medium mushrooms, sliced

Combine the vegetable oil, vinegar, sugar, dillweed, garlic salt, salt and pepper in a jar. Cover and shake to mix well.

Combine the broccoli, cauliflower, squash, carrots and mushrooms in a large bowl. Pour the dressing over the vegetables and toss to mix well. Chill, covered, for 24 hours.

Serves 10 to 12

In 1981, the Florida Legislature designated the area of Blackwater State Forest as the Canoe Capital of Florida. The many spring-fed rivers and creeks, dotted with sugar-white sand bars, meander through the pristine Blackwater Forest area and are considered the purest in the region.

Quick and Easy Yeast Rolls

1 envelope dry yeast
3/4 cup warm (105- to 115-degree) water
2 tablespoons sugar
2 tablespoons vegetable oil
1 egg
1/2 teaspoon salt
2 1/2 to 2 3/4 cups all-purpose flour
softened butter or margarine

Dissolve the yeast in the warm water in a 2 1/2-quart bowl. Add the sugar, vegetable oil, egg and salt, stirring to dissolve the sugar. Stir in 1 cup of the flour. Cover with a clean cloth and place on a rack over a bowl of hot water. Let stand for 15 minutes.

Stir down the batter and add 1 1/2 cups flour, mixing well. Knead on a floured cloth-covered board for 3 minutes, kneading in the remaining 1/4 cup flour if dough is too sticky. Shape into 16 balls and arrange in a greased 9×9-inch baking pan. Brush with softened butter. Cover with a clean cloth and place on a rack over a bowl of hot water. Let rise for 25 minutes.

Bake at 425 degrees for 12 to 15 minutes or until golden brown. Remove from the baking pan to a wire rack and brush again with softened butter.

Makes 16

Caramel-Filled Chocolate Cookies

1 cup (2 sticks) butter or margarine, softened
1 cup sugar
1 cup packed brown sugar
2 eggs
2¼ cups all-purpose flour
¾ cup baking cocoa
1 teaspoon baking soda
2 teaspoons vanilla extract
1 cup chopped pecans
1 tablespoon sugar
2 (5.3-ounce) packages chewy caramels in
  milk chocolate

Beat the butter at medium speed in a mixing bowl until creamy. Add 1 cup sugar and brown sugar gradually, beating until fluffy. Beat in the eggs.

Mix the flour, baking cocoa and baking soda together. Add to the creamed mixture and mix well. Stir in the vanilla and half the pecans. Chill, covered, for 1 hour.

Mix the remaining pecans with 1 tablespoon sugar. Press 1 tablespoon of the chilled cookie dough around each caramel, enclosing it completely. Dip 1 side of each cookie into the pecan mixture. Place the cookies pecan side up 2 inches apart on an ungreased cookie sheet.

Bake at 375 degrees for 8 minutes; cookies will still be soft. Cool on the cookie sheet for 1 minute. Remove to a wire rack to cool completely.

Makes 4 dozen

Peanut Butter and Chocolate Chunk Cookies

½ cup shortening
¾ cup sugar
⅔ cup packed brown sugar
2 egg whites
1¼ cups chunky peanut butter
1½ teaspoons vanilla extract
1 cup all-purpose flour
½ teaspoon baking soda
¼ teaspoon salt
5 (2-ounce) Butterfinger candy bars, chopped
1 cup (6 ounces) double chocolate chips

Beat the shortening in a mixing bowl until creamy. Add the sugar and brown sugar gradually, beating until fluffy. Beat in the egg whites. Add the peanut butter and vanilla and mix well.

Mix the flour, baking soda and salt together. Add to the creamed mixture and mix well. Stir in the candy pieces and chocolate chips. Shape the dough into 1½-inch balls and arrange 2 inches apart on a lightly greased cookie sheet.

Bake at 350 degrees for 11 minutes or until light golden brown. Cool on the cookie sheet for 5 minutes. Remove to a wire rack to cool completely.

Makes 4 dozen

Praline Cookies

1 2/3 cups all-purpose flour, sifted
1 1/2 teaspoons baking powder
1/2 teaspoon salt
1 1/4 cups packed light brown sugar
1 1/4 cups packed dark brown sugar
1/2 cup (1 stick) unsalted butter, softened
1 large egg
1 teaspoon vanilla extract
1/2 cup (or more) heavy cream
1 cup sifted confectioners' sugar
1 cup pecan halves, toasted, broken

Sift the flour, baking powder and salt into a medium bowl. Mix the light brown sugar and the dark brown sugar in a bowl.

Cream the butter and 1 1/2 cups of the brown sugar mixture at medium speed in a mixing bowl for 2 minutes or until light and fluffy. Beat in the egg and vanilla. Add the flour mixture and mix well at low speed.

Drop by rounded teaspoonfuls 2 inches apart on an ungreased cookie sheet. Bake at 350 degrees for 10 to 12 minutes or until golden brown. Cool in the pan on a wire rack for 5 minutes. Remove to the wire rack to cool completely.

Combine the remaining 1 cup brown sugar mixture with the cream in a small saucepan. Bring to a boil over medium heat and cook for 2 minutes, stirring constantly; remove from the heat. Whisk in the confectioners' sugar. Stir in the pecans. Adjust the consistency if necessary by adding a small amount of additional cream.

Place the cookies on the wire rack over a lined baking pan. Spoon about 1/2 teaspoon of the topping mixture over each cookie.

Makes 2 1/2 dozen

Orange Mint Lemonade

1 1/2 to 2 cups sugar
2 1/2 cups water
grated zest of 1 orange
2/3 cup orange juice
1 1/3 cups lemon juice
3/4 cup mint leaves
7 cups cold water

Bring the sugar and 2 1/2 cups water to a boil in a heavy saucepan. Reduce the heat and simmer, covered, for 5 minutes. Add the orange zest, orange juice, lemon juice and mint leaves. Let stand, covered, for 1 hour.

Strain the mixture into a 1-gallon container. Add 7 cups cold water. Chill until serving time. Serve over ice. Garnish with orange slices and mint sprigs if desired.

Makes 3 quarts

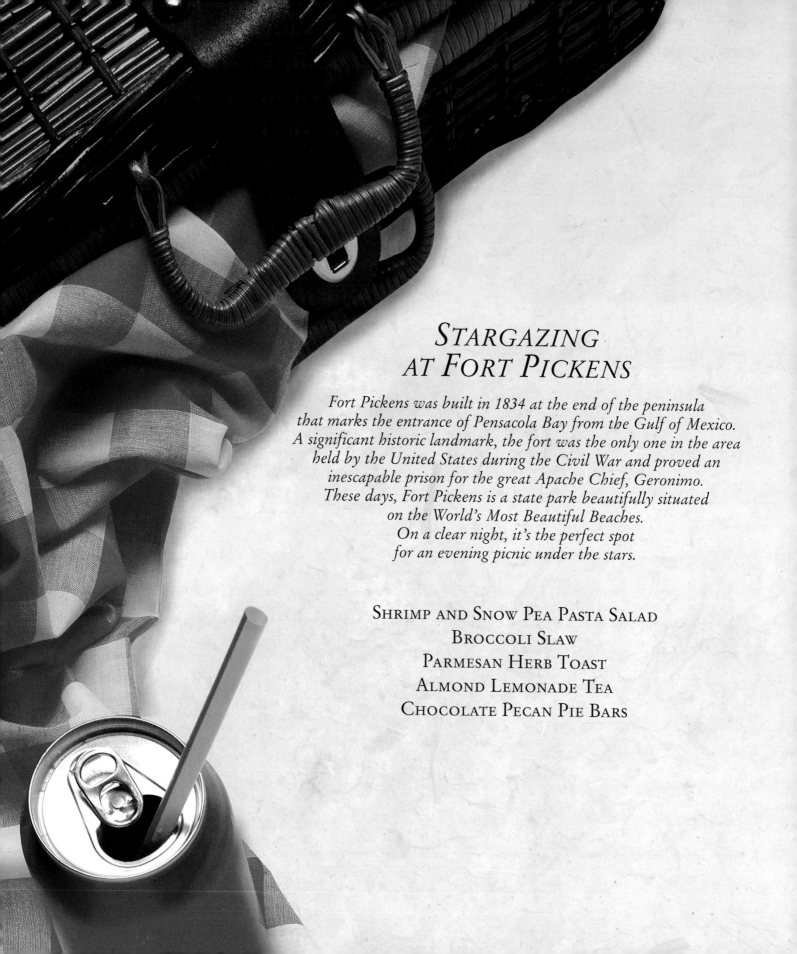

STARGAZING AT FORT PICKENS

*Fort Pickens was built in 1834 at the end of the peninsula
that marks the entrance of Pensacola Bay from the Gulf of Mexico.
A significant historic landmark, the fort was the only one in the area
held by the United States during the Civil War and proved an
inescapable prison for the great Apache Chief, Geronimo.
These days, Fort Pickens is a state park beautifully situated
on the World's Most Beautiful Beaches.
On a clear night, it's the perfect spot
for an evening picnic under the stars.*

SHRIMP AND SNOW PEA PASTA SALAD
BROCCOLI SLAW
PARMESAN HERB TOAST
ALMOND LEMONADE TEA
CHOCOLATE PECAN PIE BARS

Shrimp and Snow Pea Pasta Salad

4 1/2 cups water
1 1/2 pounds unpeeled medium fresh shrimp
16 ounces linguini
1 (6-ounce) package frozen snow peas, thawed
  and drained
6 green onions, chopped
4 medium tomatoes, peeled, chopped and drained
1/4 cup chopped fresh parsley
3/4 cup olive oil
1/3 cup wine vinegar
1 1/2 teaspoons dried basil leaves
1 teaspoon dried oregano leaves
1/2 teaspoon garlic salt
1/2 teaspoon coarsely ground pepper

Bring the water to a boil in a large saucepan. Add the shrimp and cook for 3 to 5 minutes or until the shrimp are opaque; drain and rinse with cold water to stop the cooking process. Chill in the refrigerator. Peel and devein the chilled shrimp.

Cook the linguini using the package directions, but omitting the salt. Drain the pasta, rinse with cold water and drain again.

Combine the shrimp, pasta, snow peas, green onions, tomatoes and parsley in a large bowl. Add the olive oil, vinegar, basil, oregano, garlic salt and pepper and toss gently to mix. Chill for 2 hours or longer.

You should remember never to leave shrimp or other seafood out of the refrigerator for longer than 2 hours, including the preparation and cooking time.

Serves 10

Shrimp come in many different colors. Royal red shrimp are found in the deepest water off the continental shelf and are considered the most flavorful. White shrimp are found off the coast of Florida and the Carolinas. They have a mild flavor. Pink shrimp are considered the tastiest and brown shrimp are considered the least flavorful.

Broccoli Slaw

2 packages beef-flavored ramen noodles
1 package broccoli slaw mix
1 bunch green onions, chopped
1 cup sliced almonds, toasted
1 cup dry-roasted sunflower seed kernels
3/4 cup vegetable oil
1/3 cup white vinegar
1/2 cup sugar

Crumble the ramen noodles and reserve. Combine the noodle seasoning packets with the broccoli slaw mix, green onions, almonds and sunflower seed kernels in a bowl and mix well.

Combine the vegetable oil, vinegar and sugar in a small bowl and mix well. Add to the broccoli mixture and toss to mix. Add the reserved noodles just before serving and toss gently.

Serves 20

The construction of Fort Pickens on the beach at Pensacola was completed in 1834. The Apache Indian Geronimo and 16 other Apaches were confined at Fort Pickens between 1886 and 1888, giving Pensacola its first claim to fame. At times, Geronimo's profile (at left) can still be seen at the fort.

Parmesan Herb Toast

1 cup (2 sticks) butter, softened
1/2 cup (2 ounces) grated Parmesan cheese
1 tablespoon minced garlic
1/2 tablespoon chopped fresh chives
1/2 tablespoon chopped fresh oregano
1/2 tablespoon dried basil
2 loaves French bread

Combine the butter, Parmesan cheese, garlic, chives, oregano and basil in a bowl and mix well. Cut the bread into halves horizontally and spread the cut sides with the butter mixture. Place on a baking sheet. Broil just until light brown. Cut into pieces to serve.

Serves 20

ALMOND LEMONADE TEA

Brew 4 cups of strong tea using about 6 tea bags. Add 3/4 cup sugar to the hot tea and stir to dissolve completely. Combine with 3 1/2 cups cold water, one 6-ounce can thawed frozen lemonade concentrate and 1 teaspoon almond extract in a pitcher and mix well. Chill until serving time. Serve over ice.

Chocolate Pecan Pie Bars

1 1/4 cups all-purpose flour
1/4 cup sugar
1/2 teaspoon baking powder
1/2 teaspoon cinnamon
1/2 cup (1 stick) butter
1 cup chopped pecans
1 ounce semisweet chocolate
1/4 cup (1/2 stick) butter
1 1/4 cups packed brown sugar
3 eggs, beaten
2 tablespoons bourbon or water
1 teaspoon vanilla extract

Mix the flour, sugar, baking powder and cinnamon in a bowl. Cut in 1/2 cup butter until the mixture resembles coarse crumbs. Add the pecans and mix well. Press the mixture over the bottom of an ungreased 9×13-inch baking pan. Bake at 350 degrees for 10 minutes.

Melt the chocolate and 1/4 cup butter in a small saucepan over low heat, stirring to blend well. Combine with the brown sugar, eggs, bourbon and vanilla in a small bowl and mix well. Pour over the baked layer. Bake for 20 minutes longer. Cool on a wire rack and cut into bars.

Makes 3 dozen

Effortless Entertaining

The answer to "It's just so much trouble" is "Keep it simple!" Everyone enjoys a fun party, and it may be up to you to organize one. These gatherings require very little work and rely on the help of both friends and professionals. Choose one and you'll discover that entertaining really can be effortless!

PINT-SIZED PARTY

COOKING WITH CLASS

CAJUN MADE EASY

Joe Patti's Seafood

PINT-SIZED PARTY IN THE PARK

*There's no doubt about it—children prefer time with mom at the park
more than any time-consuming food she can prepare in the kitchen.
In fact, if you put your kids in charge of a party,
the plan will probably be similar to this one. Buy some essentials ready-made
from a favorite restaurant or market and supplement with these easy, healthy recipes.
Invite your pint-sized friends and encourage them
to bring their moms for lunch at your favorite park.
No hassle—just plenty of fun for everyone!*

PIMENTO CHEESE SPREAD

PINWHEEL SANDWICHES

BLACK BEAN WRAPS

MANGO CHUTNEY CHICKEN SALAD

GREEK COUNTRY SALAD

CANDY BAR BROWNIES

KICK-THE-CAN ICE CREAM

ANTS ON A LOG

CHOCOLATE-COATED PRETZELS

SUNSHINE LEMONADE

FRUIT AND MINT ICED TEA

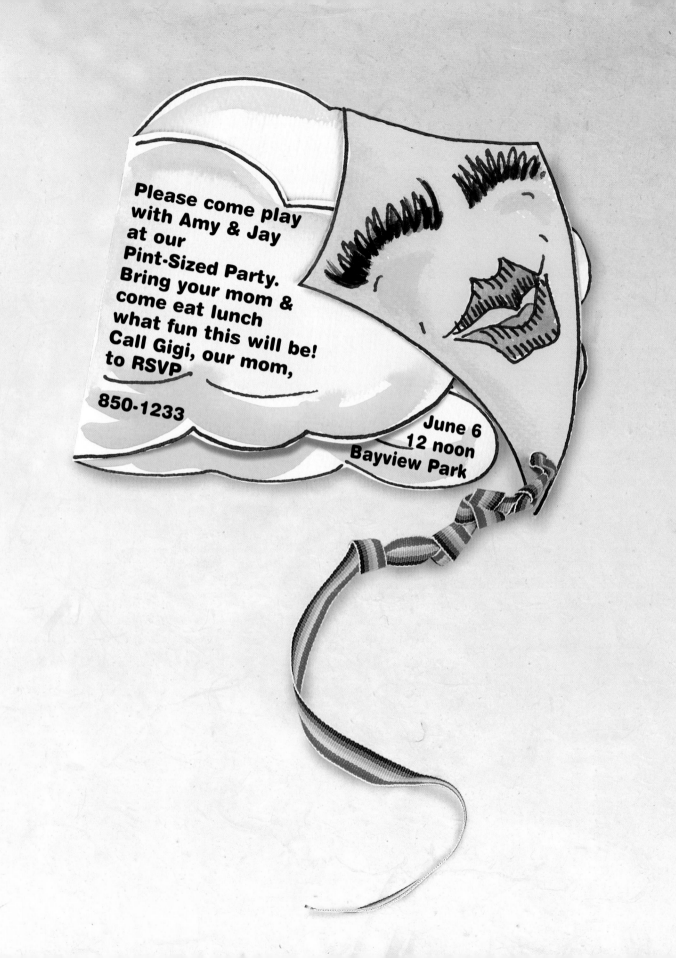

Pimento Cheese Spread

2 cups (8 ounces) sharp Cheddar cheese
1 small onion (optional)
1 teaspoon Worcestershire sauce
1 (4-ounce) jar chopped pimentos
3 (heaping) tablespoons mayonnaise
1/8 teaspoon salt
1/4 teaspoon red pepper

Combine the cheese and onion in a food processor and process until well mixed. Add the Worcestershire sauce, undrained pimentos, mayonnaise, salt and red pepper and process until smooth. Chill for 24 hours. Use as a spread for party sandwiches.

Makes 3 1/2 cups

PINWHEEL SANDWICHES

Pinwheel sandwiches are great fun for pint-size parties. They can be prepared with the Pimento Cheese Spread (above), with peanut butter or with any favorite filling. Cut the crusts from sandwich bread and flatten the bread slightly with a rolling pin. Spread with the chosen filling and roll to enclose the filling. Cut into 1-inch rounds and push a brightly-colored straw or sucker stick through the bread to create pinwheels. Tie 5 or 6 pinwheels together with a colorful ribbon and place them in sand pails to serve.

Black Bean Wraps

16 ounces cream cheese, softened
2 cups (8 ounces) shredded Pepper Jack cheese
1/2 cup sour cream
1 teaspoon onion salt
2 (15-ounce) cans black beans, rinsed and drained
1/4 cup salsa
12 (8-inch) flour tortillas
10 ounces fresh spinach
3 red bell peppers, julienned
2 carrots, shredded

Combine the cream cheese, Pepper Jack cheese, sour cream and onion salt in a mixing bowl and beat at medium speed until smooth. Process the black beans and salsa in a food processor until smooth.

Spread the bean mixture evenly over the tortillas. Spread the cheese mixture over the beans. Sprinkle with the spinach, bell peppers and carrots. Roll the tortillas tightly to enclose the filling.

Serve immediately or wrap individually in plastic wrap and chill for up to 4 hours.

Serves 12

You can have gourmet chicken salad just by adding interesting ingredients to generic chicken salad from the deli counter at the supermarket.

Try adding chopped celery and red bell pepper; chopped pecans and craisins; green grapes and pecans or almonds; crumbled crisp-cooked bacon and sour cream; lemon juice; mushrooms; green onions; cooked shell, bow-tie, or elbow pasta; chopped radishes; pineapple chunks; Dijon mustard; rosemary, or any combination you prefer. Be creative!

Mango Chutney Chicken Salad

1/2 cup mayonnaise
1/2 cup sour cream
3 tablespoons mango chutney
2 teaspoons curry powder
salt and pepper to taste
3 cups thinly sliced cooked chicken breasts
3 scallions, minced
2 ribs celery, thinly sliced
1/2 cup coarsely chopped roasted cashews
1/2 cup golden raisins

Combine the mayonnaise, sour cream, mango chutney, curry powder, salt and pepper in a large bowl and whisk until smooth.

Add the chicken, scallions, celery, cashews and raisins. Toss to coat well. Chill, covered, until serving time.

Thanks to Simply Delicious for this recipe.

Serves 8

Greek Country Salad

16 ounces feta cheese, cut into small cubes
4 cucumbers, peeled and thinly sliced
3 medium tomatoes, cut into thin wedges
1 medium red onion, thinly sliced into rings
3/4 cup Greek extra-virgin olive oil
1/4 cup Greek wine vinegar
12 large romaine leaves
1 teaspoon Greek oregano
8 anchovy fillets (optional)
16 kalamata olives
16 green olives

Combine the feta cheese, cucumbers, tomatoes and red onions in a bowl and mix gently. Add the olive oil and vinegar and toss to coat well.

Arrange the romaine leaves on a large platter. Spoon the salad mixture over the lettuce. Sprinkle with the oregano and top with the anchovies and olives.

Serves 12

Candy Bar Brownies

4 eggs, beaten
2 cups sugar
3/4 cup (11/2 sticks) margarine, melted
2 teaspoons vanilla extract
11/2 cups all-purpose flour
1/3 cup baking cocoa
1/2 teaspoon baking powder
1/4 teaspoon salt
4 (2-ounce) Snickers candy bars, coarsely chopped
3 (11/2-ounce) Hershey candy bars, coarsely chopped

Combine the eggs, sugar, margarine and vanilla in a mixing bowl and beat until smooth. Mix the flour, baking cocoa, baking powder and salt together. Add to the egg mixture and mix well. Fold in the Snickers candy.

Spoon into a greased and floured 9×13-inch baking pan. Sprinkle with the Hershey candy. Bake at 350 degrees for 30 to 35 minutes or until the brownies test done. Cool in the pan on a wire rack. Cut into squares to serve.

Makes 24

Kick-the-Can Ice Cream

1/3 cup sugar
3/4 cup milk
1 cup heavy cream
1/4 cup egg substitute
1/2 teaspoon vanilla extract
crushed ice
3/4 cup rock salt

Combine the sugar, milk, cream, egg substitute and vanilla in a bowl and mix well. Pour the mixture into a clean 1-pound coffee can with a plastic lid and seal tightly.

Place the can inside a 3-pound coffee can and fill the space between the cans with crushed ice and half the rock salt. Seal the larger can tightly with a plastic lid.

Ask children to take turns rolling the can for about 5 minutes. Drain the water from the large can and add more ice and the remaining rock salt. Seal the can again and roll the can for 10 to 15 minutes longer. Let stand for 5 minutes before serving; the ice cream will be soft.

Provide assorted candies and sprinkles and allow the children to decorate their servings.

Makes 3 cups

ANTS ON A LOG

Remove the strings from the ribs of one bunch of celery and cut the ribs into 3- to 4-inch pieces. Fill the celery with peanut butter and top with 4 or 5 raisin "ants."

Sunshine Lemonade

6 cups white grape juice
1 (12-ounce) can frozen lemonade concentrate, thawed
5 1/2 cups club soda, chilled

*C*ombine the grape juice, lemonade concentrate and club soda in a large pitcher or punch bowl and mix well. Serve over ice.

Makes 3 quarts

Fruit and Mint Iced Tea

4 cups water
8 to 10 regular tea bags
1/2 cup fresh mint leaves
1 cup sugar
1 (6-ounce) can frozen lemonade concentrate, thawed
1 (6-ounce) frozen limeade concentrate, thawed
3/4 cup orange juice
3 quarts cold water

*B*ring 4 cups water to a boil in a saucepan and add the tea bags and mint leaves. Steep, covered, for 30 minutes; discard the tea bags. Add the sugar and stir to dissolve completely.

Add the lemonade concentrate, limeade concentrate and orange juice and mix well. Strain into a large pitcher or container and add the cold water. Chill until serving time.

Makes 4 1/2 quarts

COOKING WITH CLASS

Why not make your dinner party a cooking class? Invite a local caterer or chef to turn your kitchen into a classroom for ten or twelve of your friends. The instructor, who involves your guests in the preparation of each course, plans the menu. Everyone will enjoy learning new recipes and cooking techniques. And, of course, your party is essentially effortless! Just prepare a few appetizers in advance for the "students" to enjoy while learning the chef's secrets.

CRAB AND ARTICHOKE BAKE
PESTO CHEESE TORTA
PORTOBELLO PIZZAS
PUMPKIN LOBSTER BISQUE WITH SMOKED SHRIMP
HEARTS OF PALM SALAD
BEEF EN CROÛTE WITH CORIANDER WALNUT FILLING
JOE PATTI'S OYSTERS AND PASTA
GREEN BEANS AND RED PEPPERS WITH ALMONDS
CHOCOLATE HAZELNUT BISCOTTI
FLAMBÉED FRUITS OF SUMMER
CINNAMON SPICE ICE CREAM

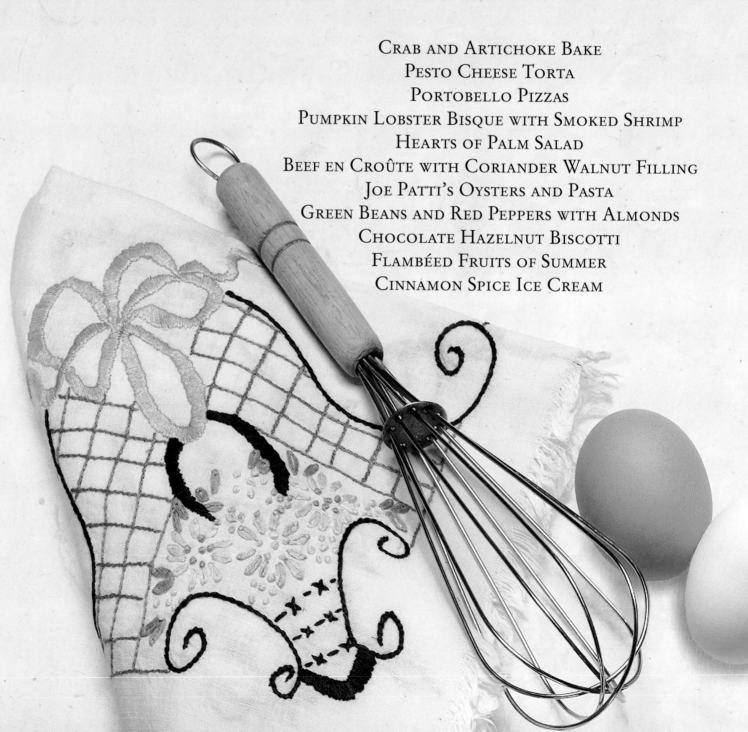

TRACY AND SCOTT'S GOURMET
GET-TOGETHER

INGREDIENTS: Good Friends and Chef Smith

COMBINE ON: Saturday, May 5th, 6 p.m.

BAKE AT: 10 Main Street

WE WILL PREPARE AND ENJOY
A NEW MENU WITH YOU!

RSVP 850-5000

BON APPETIT!

Your guests will treasure the little gifts that you send home with them to remember the evening. Have the special menu recipes already copied on pretty recipe cards and tied together with raffia. Plant aromatic herbs in small terra cotta pots wrapped in burlap and tied with raffia. Provide aprons with CWC, for Cooking with Class, to wear during the food preparation and to take home after the party.

Crab and Artichoke Bake

1 cup (2 sticks) margarine
1/3 cup minus 2 teaspoons all-purpose flour
3 cups milk
4 cups (16 ounces) shredded Pepper Jack cheese
1 medium bunch green onions, chopped
2 tablespoons finely chopped parsley
3 drops Tabasco sauce
salt and pepper to taste
2 pounds lump crab meat, flaked and drained
1 (14-ounce) can artichokes, drained and quartered
bread crumbs

Melt the margarine in a saucepan. Stir in the flour and cook until bubbly. Add the milk and cook until thickened, stirring constantly.

Add the Pepper Jack cheese, green onions, parsley, Tabasco sauce, salt and pepper and cook until the cheese melts, stirring constantly. Fold in the crab meat and artichokes.

Spoon into a 2-quart baking dish and sprinkle with bread crumbs. Bake at 350 degrees for 30 minutes. Serve as a spread with baguette slices.

Serves 16

Pesto Cheese Torta

4 garlic cloves, chopped
2 cups fresh basil leaves
1 cup virgin olive oil
1 cup (4 ounces) grated Parmesan cheese
1/4 cup (1 ounce) grated Romano cheese
1 cup walnuts or pine nuts
1/2 teaspoon each salt and pepper
32 ounces cream cheese, softened
2 tablespoons lemon juice
4 garlic cloves, chopped

Purée 4 garlic cloves with the basil in a food processor. Add the olive oil gradually, processing until smooth. Add the cheese, walnuts, salt and pepper and pulse to mix well. Mix the remaining ingredients in a bowl until smooth.

Line a 5- to 6-cup mold with two 18×18-inch squares of moistened cheesecloth. Layer half the cream cheese mixture, the pesto mixture and the remaining cream cheese mixture in the prepared mold. Fold the ends of the cheesecloth over the layers; press lightly. Chill the torte for 2 hours. Invert onto a serving plate; remove the cheesecloth.

Serves 25

SMOKED SHRIMP

Season 1 pound of tiny shrimp with salt, pepper and a small amount of sugar. Place in a lightly oiled foil cooking bag and pierce the bag in several places. Heat a smoker to a very low temperature and add hickory chips to enhance the flavor if desired. Place the cooking bag on the coolest section of the smoker and smoke for 15 minutes.

Portobello Pizzas

4 small portobello mushrooms
1/2 cup chopped spinach
1/2 cup pine nuts, toasted and coarsely chopped
1/4 cup finely chopped sun-dried tomatoes
4 garlic cloves, chopped
1/4 cup olive oil or butter
4 ounces chèvre, crumbled

Remove and chop the mushroom stems. Sauté mushroom stems, spinach, pine nuts, sun-dried tomatoes and garlic in the olive oil in a skillet until the spinach is tender. Fill mushroom caps with the sautéed mixture; arrange in a baking pan. Top with the chèvre. Bake at 350 degrees until the cheese melts. Cut into 6 wedges to serve.

Makes 24

Pumpkin Lobster Bisque

3 (or more) pinches saffron threads
1/4 cup warm water
1 large onion, chopped
1 1/2 tablespoons butter
2 ounces lobster base
6 tablespoons dry vermouth
1/2 teaspoon (or more) cayenne pepper
1 (16-ounce) can puréed pumpkin
2 tablespoons (or more) sugar
4 1/2 cups chicken broth
1 cup half-and-half
salt to taste
Smoked Shrimp (page 104)

Soak the saffron threads in the warm water. Sauté the onion in butter in a saucepan just until tender. Add saffron threads, lobster base, vermouth and cayenne pepper. Cook until the alcohol evaporates.

Stir in the pumpkin and sugar. Add the chicken broth and half-and-half gradually, stirring to blend well. Season with salt to taste and adjust the seasonings. Cook until heated through.

Place warm Smoked Shrimp in soup bowls; ladle the bisque on top. Garnish with parsley and grated lemon zest. You may purée the soup or substitute 4 1/2 cups lobster stock for the lobster base and chicken stock.

Thanks to Bob Solarski from WEAR TV3 for this recipe.

Serves 4

Hearts of Palm Salad

1/2 cup finely chopped celery
6 green olives, chopped
1/4 cup each chopped green and red bell pepper
1/4 cup finely chopped green onions
1 tablespoon dill pickle relish
1 teaspoon finely chopped garlic
1/4 teaspoon capers
3/4 cup olive oil
3 tablespoons wine vinegar
1 (16-ounce) can hearts of palm, chilled, drained
    and sliced
lettuce leaves

Combine the celery, green olives, bell peppers, green onions, pickle relish, garlic and capers in a jar. Add the olive oil and wine vinegar, cover and shake to mix well. Chill for 24 hours to blend flavors. Let stand until room temperature.

Arrange the hearts of palm on the lettuce leaves on serving plates. Spoon the dressing over the hearts of palm.

Serves 6

Beef en Croûte with Coriander Walnut Filling

CORIANDER WALNUT FILLING

2 cups walnuts
Salt to taste
1 1/2 pounds fresh spinach, trimmed
3 cups packed fresh coriander sprigs
2 cups packed fresh flat-leaf parsley sprigs
1 cup fine fresh bread crumbs
1/4 cup honey
2 egg whites
4 garlic cloves, minced
1 1/2 teaspoons salt
1 teaspoon cumin
1 teaspoon ground coriander seeds
1/4 teaspoon freshly ground pepper

BEEF

1 (4 1/2- to 5-pound) beef tenderloin, trimmed to
    about 3 inches by 16 inches
salt and pepper to taste
1 tablespoon vegetable oil
Sour Cream Pastry Dough (page 107)
1 egg
1 tablespoon water

For the filling, arrange the walnuts in a single layer in a baking pan. Toast at 350 degrees for 10 to 15 minutes or until light brown, stirring occasionally. Let stand until cool.

Add enough water to a 3-quart saucepan to fill halfway. Stir in salt and bring to a boil. Blanch the spinach in the boiling salted water for 20 seconds. Remove the spinach with a slotted spoon to a bowl of ice water to stop the cooking process. Return the salted water to a boil and add the coriander and parsley. Blanch the herbs for 5 seconds and drain in a colander. Transfer the herbs to the ice water; drain. Press the excess moisture from the spinach and herbs. Process the walnuts in a food processor until firmly ground. Add the spinach mixture, bread crumbs, honey, egg whites, garlic, salt, cumin, coriander and pepper. Pulse just until the filling is smooth. You may prepare the filling up to 2 days in advance and store, covered, in the refrigerator.

For the beef, cut the tenderloin into halves crosswise and season with salt and pepper. Heat the vegetable oil just until smoking in a large heavy skillet and brown each beef piece on all sides for 2 minutes. Remove to a platter.

Roll the pastry dough into a 15×19-inch rectangle 1/4 inch thick on a lightly floured surface. Cut a 1-inch strip from the narrower side and reserve. Arrange the rectangle on a 12×17-inch baking sheet, allowing the excess to hang over the edges.

Spread 1/3 of the filling in a 2×16-inch strip down the center of the rectangle. Place the beef pieces end to end on the filling and spread the remaining filling on the beef. Blend the egg with the water in a cup. Brush the edges of the dough with some of the egg wash.

Fold the long sides of the dough over the beef and seal the edge. Fold the ends of the dough over the wrapped beef and seal the edges. Invert a large baking sheet over the beef and invert again to place the beef seam side down. Brush with the egg wash.

Cut holly leaves and berries from the reserved dough and arrange on top, pressing gently. Brush with egg wash. Cut steam vents every 3 inches in the top of the pastry with a sharp knife. Chill, loosely covered, for 1 to 6 hours.

Insert a meat thermometer into the center of 1 piece of beef. Bake at 400 degrees in the center of the oven for 45 minutes or to 115 degrees on the meat thermometer. Let stand on the baking sheet on a rack for 35 minutes. Slice to serve.

Serves 16

Sour Cream Pastry Dough

3¼ cups all-purpose flour
1 teaspoon salt
1¼ cups (2½ sticks) unsalted butter, chilled and
    cut into ½-inch pieces
1¼ cups sour cream, chilled
4 to 6 tablespoons ice water

Combine the flour, salt and butter in a food
processor and process until the mixture resembles
coarse cornmeal. Add the sour cream and pulse
until mixed. Drizzle with 4 tablespoons water and
pulse until the mixture will hold together, adding
additional water 1 tablespoon at a time if
necessary; process the mixture as little as possible
for the most tender pastry.

Remove the dough to a work surface and divide
into 4 portions. Knead each portion until smooth.
Shape into 1 disk and wrap in plastic wrap. Chill
for 1 to 8 hours.

You may also prepare this dough by hand using
your fingers or a pastry blender. The amount of
water needed will vary depending on the humidity
and the moisture content of the butter and even
the flour.

Makes enough to wrap a 5-pound beef tenderloin

Beef tenderloins vary in shape, size and
weight. It is important for this recipe
that the tenderloin be uniform
over its length. You may find it
more satisfactory to use the center sections of
2 tenderloins.

For optimal flavor, it is best to leave
fresh herbs unwashed until time to
use them and to use them within
2 to 3 days. Cut the stems with
sharp scissors, wrap them in a damp paper
towel and store in a plastic bag or stand them
in a glass of water in the refrigerator. To dry
herbs, tie them in bunches and hang them
upside down in a cool, dark, dry place. Place
in plastic bags when completely dry. They
make good gifts to share with friends.

Joe Patti's Oysters and Pasta

1 large bunch parsley or basil, finely chopped
1 garlic clove, chopped
garlic salt to taste
1 tablespoon olive oil
2 tablespoons butter
2 pints oysters
16 ounces uncooked vermicelli or spaghetti
salt to taste
1 cup (4 ounces) grated Parmigiano-Reggiano
    cheese

Sauté the parsley and garlic with the garlic salt in
the olive oil and butter in a saucepan for 1 minute.
Add the undrained oysters. Simmer for several
minutes or just until the edges of the oysters curl,
keeping the oysters covered with liquid.

Remove the oysters from the sauce with a slotted
spoon. Cook the sauce over medium heat until
reduced to the desired consistency. Cook the pasta
al dente in salted boiling water in a saucepan; drain
partially. Ladle the pasta into serving bowls. Top with
the oysters and sauce. Sprinkle with the cheese.

Serves 8

Green Beans and Red Peppers with Almonds

1 cup sliced almonds
7 red bell peppers
2 tablespoons olive oil
2 1/2 pounds thin green beans or regular green
  beans
salt and pepper to taste

Spread the almonds in a single layer in a baking pan. Toast at 350 degrees in the center of the oven for 10 to 15 minutes or until golden brown.

Cut the bell peppers into strips 2 inches long. Sauté half the peppers in 1 tablespoon heated olive oil in a heavy 12-inch skillet for 12 minutes or until tender-crisp. Remove to a bowl and repeat with the remaining bell peppers and olive oil.

Fill a 4-quart saucepan half full with salted water and bring to a boil. Add the beans and cook for 3 to 6 minutes or until tender-crisp, depending on the size and tenderness of the beans; do not overcook.

Drain the beans and combine with the bell peppers in a bowl. Add the almonds and season with salt and pepper; toss to mix well.

Serves 16

Chocolate Hazelnut Biscotti

3/4 cup hazelnuts
4 ounces bittersweet chocolate
1/2 cup (1 stick) butter, softened
3/4 cup sugar
2 eggs
2 tablespoons Frangelico or amaretto
2 cups unbleached or all-purpose flour
1 1/2 teaspoons baking powder
1/4 teaspoon salt

Spread the hazelnuts in a single layer in a shallow baking pan and toast at 350 degrees for 8 to 10 minutes or until golden brown. Cool slightly and rub with paper towels to remove the skins. Cool to room temperature. Process in a food processor until finely ground. Remove to a bowl. Process the chocolate in a food processor until coarsely ground.

Cream the butter and sugar in a mixing bowl until light and fluffy. Beat in the eggs and liqueur. Mix the flour, baking powder and salt together. Add to the creamed mixture and mix well. Mix in the ground hazelnuts and chocolate.

Divide the dough into halves. Pat each half into a log 14 inches long, 1 1/2 inches wide and 1/2 inch thick. Place 2 inches apart on a greased and floured baking sheet. Bake in the center of the oven at 325 degrees for 25 minutes or until light brown. Remove to a wire rack to cool for 5 minutes.

Place the logs on a cutting board and slice 1/2 inch thick on a 45-degree angle. Place the slices upright 1/2 inch apart on the baking sheet. Bake for 10 minutes longer or until dry. Remove to a wire rack to cool. Store in an airtight container.

Makes 4 1/2 dozen

Flambéed Fruits of Summer

4 cups sliced peeled peaches
2 tablespoons butter
1 cup blueberries
1 cup dark sweet cherry halves
1/2 cup sugar
1/2 cup Cognac or other brandy
1/4 cup Chambord
Cinnamon Spice Ice Cream (at right)

Sauté the peaches very lightly in the butter in a large skillet over medium-high heat for 1 minute. Add the blueberries and cherries and sauté for 1 minute longer. Sprinkle with the sugar and remove from the heat.

Bring the Cognac and Chambord almost to a simmer in a small saucepan. Ignite the mixture with a long match and pour carefully over the fruit mixture. Allow the flames to subside and toss the fruit gently to coat well.

Spoon the fruit into dessert dishes. Top with scoops of Cinnamon Spice Ice Cream. Drizzle with the flambéed juices. Garnish with mint sprigs.

You may use any combination of summer fruits that you prefer and vary or omit the alcohol.

Serves 12

Cinnamon Spice Ice Cream

14 egg yolks, beaten
1 1/2 cups sugar
1 tablespoon ground cinnamon
1/2 teaspoon ground nutmeg
1/4 teaspoon ground cloves
4 cups half-and-half or light cream
3 cups heavy cream
2 teaspoons vanilla extract

Combine the egg yolks, sugar, cinnamon, nutmeg and cloves in a medium bowl and whisk until smooth. Bring the half-and-half and heavy cream to a simmer in a large saucepan over medium heat, stirring frequently.

Stir a small amount of the hot liquid into the egg yolk mixture; stir the egg yolk mixture into the hot liquid. Cook over medium-low heat just until the mixture is thickened enough to coat a metal spoon, stirring constantly. Test by drawing your finger down the center of the back of the coated spoon; if the edges of the custard hold their shape, the mixture is thickened enough.

Strain through a fine strainer into a bowl and place the bowl in a large container of ice water to cool. Stir in the vanilla and place a piece of plastic wrap directly on the surface of the custard. Chill for 2 to 24 hours.

Pour the custard into a 4- to 5-quart ice cream freezer container and freeze using the manufacturer's instructions. Remove to a chilled storage container and freeze for several hours before serving.

Makes 10 cups

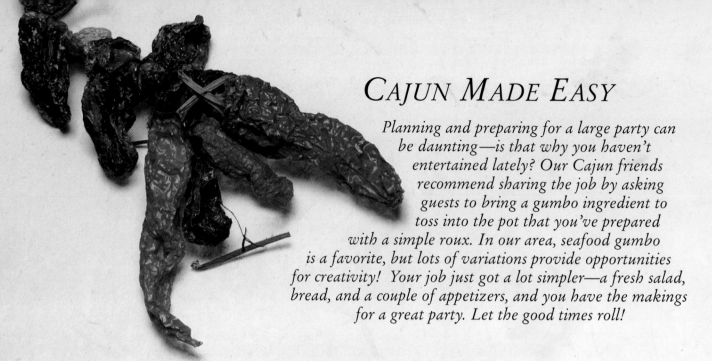

CAJUN MADE EASY

*Planning and preparing for a large party can
be daunting—is that why you haven't
entertained lately? Our Cajun friends
recommend sharing the job by asking
guests to bring a gumbo ingredient to
toss into the pot that you've prepared
with a simple roux. In our area, seafood gumbo
is a favorite, but lots of variations provide opportunities
for creativity! Your job just got a lot simpler—a fresh salad,
bread, and a couple of appetizers, and you have the makings
for a great party. Let the good times roll!*

GUMBO
CRAWFISH CORN BREAD
CAJUN HOT PUFFS
MISS FREDDIE'S SALAD
JERRY'S SHRIMP AND ANDOUILLE FETTUCINI
JIM SHIRLEY'S GRITS À YA YA
WHISKEY SOUR SLUSH
EASY ETOUFFÉE
BREAD PUDDING WITH CHOCOLATE AND PECANS

Gumbo

1 pound unpeeled shrimp
2 quarts water
3 large onions, chopped
1 bell pepper, chopped
2 cups finely chopped celery
3 garlic cloves, crushed
salt and pepper to taste
Roux (at right)
1 (16-ounce) can tomatoes
4 bay leaves, crushed
2 cups thinly sliced okra
8 ounces crab meat
1 pint oysters
Worcestershire sauce and hot sauce to taste
hot cooked rice

Peel the shrimp, reserving the heads and peels. Combine the heads and peels with the water in a saucepan. Bring to a simmer and simmer for 15 minutes. Strain and reserve the stock.

Add the onions, bell pepper, celery, garlic, salt and pepper to the Roux in a heavy cast-iron skillet. Cook until the vegetables are tender, stirring constantly. Stir in the reserved shrimp stock. Cook until thickened, stirring constantly. Add the tomatoes and bay leaves.

Bring to a boil and reduce the heat. Simmer, covered, for 1 hour. Stir in the okra, shrimp and crab meat. Simmer just until the seafood and okra are tender. Add the oysters, Worcestershire sauce and hot sauce; adjust the seasonings. Cook just until the edges of the oysters begin to curl. Serve over rice.

Serves 8

It is easy to decorate for this party. You can sometimes find fabric printed with crawfish and bottles of hot sauce to use for tablecloths. Otherwise just use informal tablecloths or cover the tables with white paper. Use rustic lanterns with candles, wicker fishing baskets, bottles of hot sauce and gumbo filé for table decorations, and large buckets to ice beer and soft drinks. Small bottles of hot sauce make nice favors.

Roux

1/2 cup vegetable oil
1/2 cup all-purpose flour

Heat the vegetable oil in a heavy cast-iron skillet. Stir in the flour carefully to avoid spattering. Cook over low heat until the mixture is dark brown for gumbo, stirring constantly.

You may also heat the dry flour in a skillet until it is light brown, then stir in the oil and continue to cook until it reaches the desired color. To microwave, combine the flour and oil in a microwave-safe dish and mix well. Microwave on High until the mixture reaches the desired color, stirring every minute.

To avoid burning a roux, always use a heavy skillet and do not substitute butter for the oil. Discard a roux if it does begin to burn, as the taste will be bitter and will ruin the gumbo.

Makes 3/4 cup

Crawfish Corn Bread

1 cup cornmeal
1/2 teaspoon baking soda
1 teaspoon salt
3 eggs, lightly beaten
1/3 cup vegetable oil
1 (16-ounce) can cream-style corn
1 medium onion, chopped
1 cup (4 ounces) grated Parmesan cheese
1 cup (4 ounces) shredded Cheddar cheese
1/3 cup finely chopped jalapeño peppers
1 pound crawfish tails, cooked

Mix the cornmeal, baking soda and salt together. Combine the eggs, vegetable oil and corn in a mixing bowl and mix well. Stir in the onion, Parmesan cheese, Cheddar cheese, and jalapeño peppers. Add the cornmeal mixture and mix well. Stir in the crawfish tails.

Spoon into a greased 9×13-inch baking pan. Bake at 375 degrees for 30 minutes or until golden brown. Serve warm.

Serves 12

Cajun Hot Puffs

1 (17-ounce) package frozen puff pastry, thawed
8 ounces hot smoked link sausage
1/3 cup sliced jalapeño peppers, drained

Roll each pastry sheet into a 12×15-inch rectangle on a work surface lightly sprinkled with cornmeal. Cut into 3-inch squares. Cut the sausage into slices 1/4 inch thick. Place 1 slice of sausage and 1 slice of jalapeño pepper on each pastry square. Fold the corners to the center, overlapping the edges to enclose the filling.

Place the filled pastries seam side down on a greased baking sheet sprinkled with additional cornmeal. Bake at 400 degrees for 12 to 15 minutes or until golden brown.

You may prepare the filled pastries and freeze in an airtight container for up to 3 months before baking.

Makes 40

Miss Freddie's Salad

1 package chopped romaine
1 package musclun
1 red bell pepper, thinly sliced
1 green bell pepper, thinly sliced
1 small jar pepperoncini, drained
1 (16-ounce) jar artichoke hearts, drained and
   chopped
1 (8-ounce) can pitted medium black olives,
   drained
1 small jar capers, drained
croutons
grated Parmesan cheese to taste
sunflower seed kernels to taste
alfalfa sprouts to taste
1 (16-ounce) bottle Caesar Parmesan salad
   dressing

Combine the romaine, mesclun, bell peppers, pepperoncini, artichoke hearts, black olives and capers in a large bowl.

Top with croutons, Parmesan cheese, sunflower seed kernels and alfalfa sprouts. Add the salad dressing and toss to coat well.

Serves 12

Jerry's Shrimp and Andouille Fettucini

2 tablespoons butter
8 ounces andouille sausage, chopped
12 ounces (31- to 35-count) peeled shrimp, deveined
1 teaspoon minced garlic
1/4 cup chopped green onions
1/4 cup freshly squeezed lemon juice
1 tablespoon (or more) Seafood Magic
1 tablespoon Jerry's ZydeCajun seasoning
1 teaspoon each dried basil and dried thyme
1/2 teaspoon Melinda's Habanero Sauce (optional)
4 cups cooked and drained fettucini
1 cup half-and-half
1 cup (4 ounces) shredded provolone cheese
1/2 cup (2 ounces) grated Parmesan cheese
3/4 cup chopped green onions

Heat the butter in a skillet over medium heat. Add the andouille, shrimp, garlic and 1/4 cup green onions and sauté until the shrimp are nearly cooked through. Stir in the lemon juice, 1 tablespoon Seafood Magic, Jerry's ZydeCajun seasoning, basil, thyme and Habanero sauce.

Reduce the heat and add the pasta and half-and-half. Cook until heated through. Sprinkle with the cheeses and cook until the cheeses melt, stirring constantly. Stir in 3/4 cup green onions and additional Seafood Magic if desired.

Add additional half-and-half if the sauce appears too thick and cheese if it is too thin. Spoon into a serving bowl. Garnish with additional provolone cheese, green onions and Seafood Magic.

Thanks to Jerry Mistretta of Jerry's Cajun Café for this recipe.

Serves 6

Jim Shirley's Grits à Ya Ya

8 slices bacon, chopped
1 tablespoon chopped shallots
1 tablespoon minced garlic
3 tablespoons butter
1 bottle of wine, preferably Spanish wine
1 pound peeled jumbo shrimp
2 cups chopped spinach
1 cup chopped portabello mushrooms
1/4 cup sliced scallions
2 cups heavy cream
hot sauce, salt and pepper to taste
3 cups cooked smoked Gouda cheese grits

Cook the bacon in a large saucepan over medium heat for 3 minutes or until the drippings are rendered. Add 1 tablespoon shallots and garlic and sauté until tender. Add the butter and a splash of the wine and cook until the butter begins to melt. Pour the rest of the wine for the guests helping you cook.

Add the shrimp and sauté until the shrimp are cooked through, turning to cook evenly. Stir in the spinach, mushrooms and 1/4 cup scallions. Sauté for 2 minutes longer. Remove the shrimp with a slotted spoon.

Add the cream and simmer until reduced by 1/3. Season with hot sauce, salt and pepper. Return the shrimp to the saucepan and cook until heated through. Serve over the grits.

Thanks to Jim Shirley of the Fish House restaurant for this recipe.

Serves 4

Easy Etouffée

1 each red and green bell pepper, chopped
1 onion, chopped
4 ribs celery, chopped
2 tablespoons minced garlic
1 (4-ounce) jar pimentos, drained
1 cup (2 sticks) butter
2 (10-ounce) cans cream of mushroom soup
1 can beer
1 tablespoon fresh lemon juice
2 tablespoons ketchup
1 tablespoon Worcestershire sauce
salt, red pepper and black pepper to taste
2 pounds frozen crawfish tails
hot cooked rice

Sauté the bell peppers, onion, celery, garlic and pimentos in the butter in a large saucepan until tender. Add the soup, beer, lemon juice, ketchup and Worcestershire sauce. Simmer for 10 minutes, stirring constantly. Season with salt, red pepper and black pepper. Add the crawfish. Cook over medium-low heat for 30 minutes. Serve over rice.

You may prepare this dish ahead and reheat. Frozen vegetables may be substituted for the fresh vegetables.

Serves 8

Bread Pudding with Chocolate and Pecans

1 cup whipping cream
1/2 cup sugar
1/4 cup sour cream
2 teaspoons Triple Sec
1 teaspoon vanilla extract
6 large eggs
2 1/2 cups sugar
1/2 cup (1 stick) unsalted butter, melted
2 1/2 teaspoons ground nutmeg
2 1/2 teaspoons ground cinnamon
1 tablespoon vanilla extract
4 cups cream
4 cups milk
1 cup coarsely chopped roasted pecans
1 cup (6 ounces) semisweet chocolate chips
10 cups torn stale bread with crusts

Beat the cream in a mixing bowl until it begins to thicken. Add 1/2 cup sugar, sour cream, liqueur and 1 teaspoon vanilla and beat until soft peaks form. Store in the refrigerator.

Beat the eggs in a mixing bowl for 3 minutes. Add 2 1/2 cups sugar, butter, nutmeg, cinnamon and 1 tablespoon vanilla and mix well. Beat in the cream and milk. Stir in the pecans and chocolate chips.

Sprinkle the bread in a greased 11×16-inch baking pan. Pour the egg mixture over the bread. Let stand for 45 minutes.

Place in an oven preheated to 350 degrees. Reduce the oven temperature to 300 degrees and bake for 40 minutes. Increase the oven temperature to 425 degrees and bake for 15 to 20 minutes or until puffed and golden brown. Top servings with whipped cream.

Serves 15

Entertaining Outdoors

Moving the party outdoors can be the solution to entertaining obstacles such as space constraints. Outside parties also provide opportunities for creative staging and decorating! The ideas in this section are easily adaptable to a variety of occasions and are sure memory-makers.

GHOST AWAKENING

MIDSUMMER'S EVE

SAFARI SEND-OFF

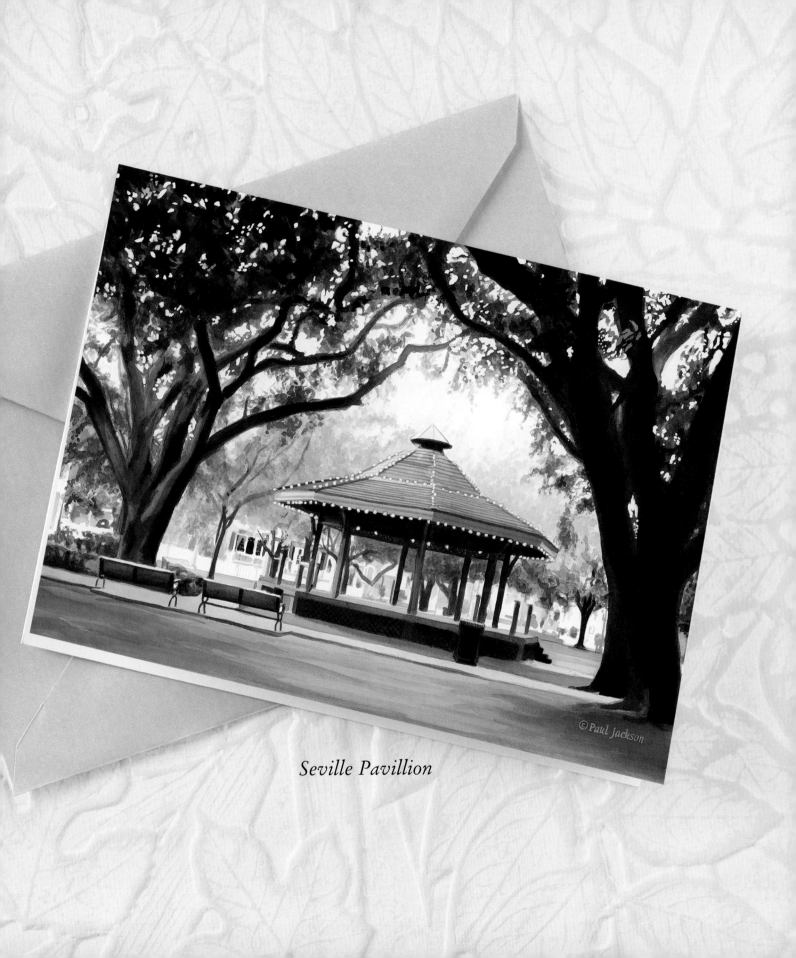

Seville Pavillion

©Paul Jackson

GHOST AWAKENING

*Southerners have never gotten so practical that we dismiss something
(or someone) just because it (or she) can't be explained.
Although our friends in St. Augustine, Florida, claim the oldest **continuous** settlement,
Pensacola was settled first. So, perhaps our long history and preservationist spirit
can explain our fascination with ghosts and their stories.
Between heavy hors d'oeuvres and decadent desserts, take your friends
on an evening tour of your local ghost haunts. Boo!*

FAKE BAKED BRIE
FATAL FETA CHEESE MELT
LADY'S FINGERS
COFFIN DIP
BLACK CAT CHEESE SPREAD
RUBBED BONES WITH SPICY BLACK FRUIT SAUCE
IMPS ON HORSEBACK
FRIGHTFUL CRAB MOLD
BAT TONGUES
DEVIL'S EYES
WITCH'S WARTS
SCARY BERRY PIE
DIABLO'S FAVORITE DESSERT
ZOMBIE BREW
IRISH WAKE COFFEE

Ghost stories are a traditional part of the celebration of Halloween, the eve of All Saints Day and the beginning of the Celtic new year. It was said that souls of the dead visited their homes on this day. In Pensacola, the devout Spaniards observed the custom of burning candles in St. Michael's cemetery on All Saints Eve; the candle, considered an emblem of purification, was placed on the graves as a prayer for the soul of the buried person.

Your town probably has some interesting ghost stories, or you can use some of these from Pensacola's past, found in *Ghosts, Legends and Folklore of Old Pensacola* by Sandra Johnson and Leora Sutton.

SARAH WHARTON

Sarah and her father were captured by a band of pirates. After killing her father, the pirate captain turned to put his arms around Sarah to kiss her. She seized the opportunity to strike him with the hand that bore a rather large diamond. The ring tore out one of the pirate's eyes and damaged the other. In a fit of pain and passion, the pirate swung his cutlass and severed the head from the body of beautiful Sarah. This tall graceful girl has since been seen wandering along Romano Street near the water. Reflections from her ring sparkle when the moonlight strikes the hand of her headless figure.

JUAN ALVERADO

Juan was a Spanish soldier who, with a friend, was exploring the Escambia River, guided by some Indians who were supposedly friendly. The Indians turned on the Spaniards, killing the friend outright and mortally wounding Juan, who hid in the hollow of a cypress tree, but lacked the strength to get out. Settlers sighted an armored ghost at sunset once a year. In 1929, the tree was cut down, revealing the skeleton wearing a suit of armor. The ghost has not been seen since Juan's remains were buried in a cemetery.

PAULINE CHARBONIER

Pauline and her sister, Dolores, are said to haunt the Charbonier House (at left) on the corner of Intendencia and Florida Blanca. The reclusive sisters shared the residence for many years, growing up there with their parents and two brothers, both of whom died tragically. Imogene Kennedy, a Junior League sustainer, now lives there and reports numerous sightings of Pauline and, possibly, her sister within the walls of the house.

THOMAS MORISTO

The ghost of the Gray House at 314 Alcaniz Street is said to still move things around at night when the offices that the building now contains are closed. Thomas was a sea captain who returned home to find his sweetheart gone and his home partially destroyed by fire. His name was discovered by a resident using a Ouija™ board. The ghost gave 1718 as his birth date and 1803 as his date of death. A medium visiting Pensacola who had not been given Thomas' name later held a séance in the home and confirmed the name and dates.

CLARA BARKLEY DORR

The Dorr House, located off Seville Square, was built by Clara, the widow of Eben Dorr, the territorial sheriff. Guides who give tours of the house have seen shadows and find things moved. Another felt someone tug on her skirt. A neighbor reported that the alarm at the house went off before the power was connected to it.

JEREMIAH INGRAHAM

Jeremiah, the first keeper of the Naval Air Station lighthouse, is said to laugh at people and slam doors. Items left downstairs will sometimes be found upstairs.

ARCHIE MOONLIGHT

Archie was a ghost who frequented Seville Square in June of 1888 and was said to have the power to contract and expand at will. Some people reported that he wore armor and clanked when he walked. He had the playful habit of doing back summersaults over fences, and enjoyed scaring the people who came looking for him.

CURIOUS BLUE LIGHT

The Old Axelson House (above) is located at the corner of Florida Blanca and Zarragossa streets. This house was occupied by two cousins, Margaret Axelson and Margaret Cromarty. After the death of Margaret Axelson in 1940, a curious blue light appeared in a downstairs bedroom window. This blinking light appeared only at night. During war times, there were very strict laws regarding lights after dark. It was said that even the light of a cigarette was forbidden. Because of the strict rules of the time, neighborhood watch groups reported the strange light to officials. After many weeks of observation, the light's origin could not be explained and left officials dumbfounded. The light continued to be seen until the fall of 1953 and has never been seen again.

Fake Baked Brie is contributed by Mary Proctor, the artist of the invitations used in the book. Fatal Feta Cheese Melt is contributed by Barrett McClean, the photographer. Read about them on page 5.

Fake Baked Brie

2 (15-count) packages miniature phyllo shells
1 small round Brie cheese
10 tablespoons chutney
30 almond slices
1 cup packed brown sugar

Remove the plastic wrapping from the miniature phyllo shells but leave the shells in the plastic liner. Place 1 teaspoon cheese into each shell and top each with 1 teaspoon chutney, 1 almond slice and 1/2 teaspoon brown sugar.

Remove the filled shells to a baking sheet and bake at 350 degrees for 5 minutes. Serve warm.

You may vary the ingredients, using apricot jam, peach jam, light brown sugar, dried cranberries, mushrooms, pecans or other ingredients to suit your taste.

Makes 30

Fatal Feta Cheese Melt

1/2 cup (1 stick) margarine, softened
2 teaspoons crushed or finely chopped garlic
1 loaf sliced Italian bread
1 container feta or seasoned feta, crumbled
4 Roma tomatoes, thinly sliced

Combine the margarine and garlic in a small bowl and mix well. Spread over 1 side of the bread slices and arrange on a baking sheet. Sprinkle with the feta cheese and top with the tomato slices. Broil just until the cheese melts. Serve immediately.

Serves 16

LADY'S FINGERS

Trim the tough ends from 1 bunch of thin asparagus. Cook in boiling water in a saucepan just until tender-crisp; drain and plunge into cold water to stop the cooking process. Trim the crusts from a loaf of sliced Pepperidge Farm white bread and roll the slices flat. Spread with a mixture of 4 ounces softened Danish bleu cheese and 4 ounces softened cream cheese. Arrange 1 asparagus spear on each slice of bread, leaving the tips exposed and roll the bread to enclose the asparagus. Cover with plastic wrap and chill until serving time.

Coffin Dip

10 Roma tomatoes, chopped
1/2 cup chopped purple onion or Vidalia onion
3 to 6 green onions, chopped
2 teaspoons minced garlic
1 tablespoon olive oil
2 tablespoons balsamic vinegar
2 tablespoons white wine vinegar
1 tablespoon sugar
1/4 teaspoon salt
1/4 teaspoon pepper
1 cup (4 ounces) crumbled feta cheese
French bread, thinly sliced

Combine the tomatoes, chopped onion, green onions and garlic in a bowl. Add the olive oil, balsamic vinegar, wine vinegar, sugar, salt and pepper and mix well. Sprinkle with the feta cheese.

Cut the bread into coffin shapes and arrange on a baking sheet. Broil until toasted. Serve with the dip.

Serves 12

Black Cat Cheese Spread

1 garlic clove
16 ounces cream cheese, softened
1 cup (2 sticks) margarine, softened
1 tablespoon chopped fresh oregano
1 teaspoon chopped fresh basil
1 teaspoon chopped fresh dill
1 teaspoon chopped fresh thyme
1/4 teaspoon dried marjoram
1/2 cup coarsely ground peppercorns
3 black licorice strips
1 red bell pepper

Purée the garlic in a food processor, scraping down the side once. Add the cream cheese, margarine, oregano, basil, dill, thyme and marjoram and process until smooth. Chill for 1 hour.

Shape into a cat on a serving platter. Cover with the ground peppercorns. Add licorice strips for whiskers and cut red bell pepper eyes and nose. Chill until serving time. Serve with crackers.

Serves 12

Rubbed Bones with
Spicy Black Fruit Sauce

SPICY BLACK FRUIT SAUCE

1 tablespoon unsalted butter
2 tablespoons finely chopped red onion
1 tablespoon finely chopped roasted garlic
1 teaspoon minced seeded jalapeño pepper
1/2 cup port
1 1/2 cups red wine
1 cup chicken stock
1/4 cup thawed grape juice concentrate
1/2 cup sliced seedless black grapes
1/2 cup fresh or frozen raspberries
salt and freshly ground pepper to taste

RIBS

2 (8-chop) French-cut racks of lamb
1/4 cup olive oil
2 teaspoons each ground cumin and rosemary
salt and pepper to taste

For the sauce, melt the butter in a saucepan over medium heat. Add the onion, garlic and jalapeño pepper and sauté for 5 minutes. Increase the heat to high and add the port. Cook for 10 minutes or until the port is reduced to 1 tablespoon. Add the red wine and cook for 10 minutes or until reduced to 1 tablespoon.

Add the chicken stock and grape juice concentrate. Cook until the liquid is reduced to 1/3. Stir in the grapes and raspberries; season with salt and pepper.

For the ribs, slice the lamb racks into chops, leaving the bone. Coat the chops with the olive oil and rub with the cumin, rosemary, salt and pepper. Place in a roasting pan. Roast at 350 degrees for 15 minutes or until cooked through. Serve with the sauce.

Serves 8

Frightful Crab Mold

1 envelope unflavored gelatin
1/4 cup cold water
1/2 cup condensed cream of shrimp soup
4 ounces cream cheese
1/2 cup mayonnaise
1 tablespoon lemon juice
1 tablespoon Worcestershire sauce
1 tablespoon Tabasco sauce
4 ounces lump crab meat
1/4 cup chopped onion
1/4 cup chopped celery
1/4 cup chopped green bell pepper

Soften the gelatin in the water in a cup. Combine the soup and cream cheese in a saucepan and heat until the cream cheese melts, stirring to blend well. Add the gelatin mixture, stirring until completely dissolved. Remove from the heat.

Stir in the mayonnaise, lemon juice, Worcestershire sauce and Tabasco sauce. Add the remaining ingredients and mix well. Spoon into a mold and chill until firm. Unmold onto a serving plate and serve with melba toast rounds.

Serves 8

Bat Tongues

1/2 cup olive oil
2 tablespoons fresh lemon juice
1 tablespoon honey
1 tablespoon soy sauce
2 tablespoons chopped fresh parsley
2 tablespoons Cajun seasoning
1/4 teaspoon cayenne pepper
1 pound peeled uncooked large shrimp

Combine the olive oil, lemon juice, honey, soy sauce, parsley, Cajun seasoning and cayenne pepper in a bowl and mix well. Add the shrimp and toss to coat well. Chill for 1 hour.

Spoon into a baking dish. Bake at 450 degrees for 10 minutes or until the shrimp are cooked through. Serve with French bread.

Serves 4

DEVIL'S EYES

Peel 24 hard-cooked eggs and cut them into halves lengthwise. Separate the yolks from the whites. Combine the egg yolks with 3 tablespoons mayonnaise or sour cream, 2 teaspoons Dijon mustard, 4 finely chopped scallions, 4 drops Tabasco sauce, 2 teaspoons curry powder, 1/4 teaspoon white pepper and salt to taste in a bowl; mix well. Spoon into the egg whites and top with a slice of black olive. Spoon red caviar into the centers of the olive slices to resemble bloodshot eyes. Chill until serving time.

Witch's Warts

1 small red bell pepper
2 plum tomatoes, chopped
1 cup chopped onion
2 garlic cloves
1/4 teaspoon dried crushed red pepper
8 ounces oil-pack sun-dried tomatoes, drained
    and cut into strips
3/4 cup water
1/4 cup heavy cream
1/4 cup red wine vinegar
3 tablespoons fresh lemon juice
1/3 cup vegetable oil
1 pound fresh mushrooms

Cut the bell pepper into halves lengthwise. Place cut side down on a baking sheet. Broil until evenly charred. Place in a paper bag and let stand for 10 minutes. Remove and discard the peel and chop the bell pepper coarsely.

Combine the bell pepper with the plum tomatoes, onion, garlic and red pepper in a food processor and process until smooth. Remove to a medium bowl.

Combine the sun-dried tomatoes, water, heavy cream, vinegar and lemon juice in the food processor and process until smooth. Add the vegetable oil gradually, processing constantly until smooth.

Whisk the sun-dried tomato mixture into the fresh tomato mixture and mix well. Add the mushrooms. Chill in the refrigerator for 8 hours or longer. Serve with wooden picks.

Serves 8

Scary Berry Pie

1 (1-crust) flaky pie pastry
2 large eggs
3/4 cup packed light brown sugar
3/4 cup pure maple syrup
2 tablespoons unsalted butter, melted
1 teaspoon vanilla extract
1/4 teaspoon salt
2 cups coarsely chopped walnuts
1 cup coarsely chopped fresh cranberries

Fit the pastry into a buttered 9-inch glass pie plate; trim and crimp the edge. Freeze for 15 minutes.

Beat the eggs with the brown sugar in a large mixing bowl. Whisk in the maple syrup, butter, vanilla and salt. Stir in the walnuts and cranberries. Spoon into the prepared pastry.

Bake at 400 degrees on a rack in the bottom third of the oven for 10 minutes. Reduce the oven temperature to 350 degrees and bake for 35 minutes longer or until the filling is set. Cool to room temperature and serve with whipped cream.

Serves 8

Diablo's Favorite Dessert

BROWNIE CRUST

2 teaspoons coffee granules
1/3 cup hot water
2 cups light fudge brownie mix
2 egg whites
1 teaspoon vanilla extract

FILLING

3/4 cup low-fat milk
2 tablespoons Kahlúa or other coffee liqueur
1 teaspoon coffee granules
1 package chocolate instant pudding mix
1 teaspoon vanilla extract
3 cups whipped topping
1 teaspoon coffee granules
1 tablespoon Kahlúa or other coffee liqueur

For the crust, dissolve the coffee granules in the hot water in a medium bowl. Add the brownie mix, egg whites and vanilla and stir to mix well. Spoon into a 9-inch pie plate sprayed with nonstick cooking spray. Bake at 325 degrees for 22 minutes. Cool on a wire rack.

For the filling, combine the milk, 2 tablespoons Kahlúa, 1 teaspoon coffee granules, pudding mix and vanilla in a mixing bowl. Beat at medium speed for 1 minute. Fold in half of the whipped topping. Spread over the crust.

Combine 1 teaspoon coffee granules with 1 tablespoon Kahlúa in a mixing bowl and mix well. Fold in the remaining whipped topping. Spread over the pudding mixture. Serve immediately or chill until serving time. Garnish with chocolate curls if desired.

Serves 8

IRISH WAKE COFFEE

Combine 1 cup freshly made coffee with 1 jigger of Irish whiskey and 1 to 2 teaspoons light brown sugar for every serving in a saucepan. Bring just to a simmer and pour into cups, filling to within 1/2 inch of the rim. Top each with a dollop of whipped cream and sprinkle with baking cocoa; garnish with chocolate sticks.

ZOMBIE BREW

Combine 10 cups unsweetened pineapple juice with 9 cups cranberry juice cocktail, 4 1/2 cups water and 1 cup packed brown sugar in a 30-cup coffeemaker. Combine 4 cinnamon sticks, 4 teaspoons whole cloves and 1/2 teaspoon salt in the basket. Perk through a regular cycle. Serve hot or cold. You may add vodka if desired.

MIDSUMMER'S EVE

While Southerners spend the long, hot days of summer hiding from the sun, outdoor evenings can be magical. The longest day of the year in the northern hemisphere, the summer solstice, occurs in late June. Take some tips from Mr. Shakespeare's play and transform your backyard into a forest fantasyland. Encourage guests to dress the part— cool, lightweight fabrics that are comfortable and reminiscent of fairies and free spirits would be just what the bard ordered!

SPICY ARTICHOKE DIP

BLEU CHEESE FONDUE

OPEN-FACED PESTO AND MUSHROOM SANDWICHES

SUN-DRIED TOMATO AND CHEDDAR SANDWICHES

CHICKEN SALAD FINGER SANDWICHES WITH ROASTED PECANS

SNAKE IN THE GARDEN

OYSTERS MOSCA

BLACK FOREST CAKE

FROZEN BUTTERMILK

DREAM COOKIES

Midsummer's Eve

Be merry with me, come sing and dance
This night that equals day—June 21st
A magic night in whose length
Elves frolic, light and prance
7 o'clock this evening until when...
 At my house—this forest glen
 Where chance we love and chance we see
 How happy our lives can be!

 Be my guest as we celebrate
 The magical summer solstice!
 Tammy Rogers
 850-2121

Transform your yard into a fairyland for this event. Use twinkling lights and lanterns in the trees, wreaths, and flowers, mystical music and tables covered with clear iridescent mylar and candles. Glow-in-the-dark necklaces should be given to guests to wear during the evening. The 1920s movie version of Shakespeare's *A Midsummer Night's Dream* could project through the crowd onto a sheet suspended between trees and signs might include quotations from the play, such as:

"Stir up the Athenian youth
    to merriments;
Awake the pert and nimble
    spirit of mirth;
Turn melancholy forth to
    funerals;
The pale companion is not
    for our pomp."

"And we fairies that do run
    By the triple Hecate's team
From the presence of the sun,
    Following darkness like a dream,
Now are frolic; . . ."

Spicy Artichoke Dip

1 (14-ounce) can artichoke hearts, drained
1 cup (4 ounces) grated Parmesan cheese
1/2 cup each sour cream and mayonnaise
8 ounces cream cheese, softened
2 garlic cloves, minced
2 jalapeño peppers, seeded and chopped
1/2 teaspoon salt

Combine the artichoke hearts, Parmesan cheese, sour cream, mayonnaise, cream cheese, garlic, jalapeño peppers and salt in a food processor and process until smooth.

Spread in a 9-inch baking dish. Bake at 325 degrees for 30 to 45 minutes or until light brown. Serve with pita triangles.

Serves 10

Bleu Cheese Fondue

1 cup milk
8 ounces cream cheese, cubed and softened
8 ounces Danish bleu cheese, crumbled
1 tablespoon corn flour
1/2 teaspoon garlic salt
2 tablespoons cream

Combine the milk and cream cheese in a mixing bowl and beat until smooth. Spoon into a fondue pot over low heat and heat until the cream cheese melts. Add the bleu cheese gradually. Heat and stir constantly until smooth.

Blend the corn flour and garlic salt with the cream in a cup. Add to the cheese mixture and heat until thickened and creamy, stirring constantly. Serve with cubes of crusty bread and sliced pears.

Serves 8

Open-Faced Pesto and Mushroom Sandwiches

1 cup fresh basil leaves
1 cup fresh cilantro leaves
2 tablespoons pine nuts, toasted
1 tablespoon grated Parmesan cheese
4 garlic cloves
1/4 cup extra-virgin olive oil
1 tablespoon lemon juice
1/2 teaspoon each salt and pepper
8 ounces fresh mushrooms, thinly sliced
1 baguette
mayonnaise

Combine the basil, cilantro, pine nuts, Parmesan cheese, garlic, olive oil, lemon juice, salt and pepper in a food processor and process until well mixed. Combine the puréed mixture with the mushrooms in a skillet and sauté until the mushrooms are tender.

Slice the baguette into 1/4-inch slices. Spread lightly with mayonnaise and top with the pesto and mushroom mixture. Serve immediately.

Makes 4 dozen

SUN-DRIED TOMATO AND CHEDDAR SANDWICHES

Trim the crusts from 1 loaf of thinly sliced pumpernickel bread. Combine 2 cups finely shredded Cheddar cheese with 1/4 cup minced sun-dried tomatoes and 3 tablespoons mayonnaise in a bowl and mix well. Spread on half the bread slices and top with the remaining bread. Slice diagonally into 4 triangles.

Chicken Salad Finger Sandwiches with Roasted Pecans

3 cups finely chopped cooked chicken breasts
3/4 cup chopped roasted pecans
1 (20-ounce) can crushed pineapple, drained
1 cup finely chopped celery
1/3 cup yogurt
1 teaspoon ground ginger
salt and pepper to taste
1/3 cup (or more) mayonnaise
1 loaf thinly sliced sandwich bread
1/3 cup mayonnaise
green tops of 1 bunch scallions, minced

Combine the chicken, pecans, pineapple, celery, yogurt, ginger, salt and pepper in a bowl. Add 1/3 cup mayonnaise or enough to make of the desired consistency and mix well. Chill in the refrigerator.

Trim the crusts from the bread. Spread half the slices with the chicken salad and top with the remaining slices. Cut each sandwich into 3 fingers.

Spread the edges of the sandwiches with 1/3 cup mayonnaise and dip in the scallion tops to coat evenly. Chill, covered, until serving time.

Makes 3 dozen

Oysters Mosca

4 dozen oysters with liquor
1 large onion, finely chopped
2 tablespoons butter
3 garlic cloves, finely chopped, or
   1 teaspoon garlic powder
3/4 teaspoon oregano
1/2 teaspoon thyme
salt and pepper to taste
1 cup seasoned bread crumbs
grated Parmesan cheese

Drain the oysters, reserving the liquid. Sauté the onion in the butter in a skillet. Add the oysters, garlic, oregano, thyme, salt and pepper. Sauté until the edges of the oysters begin to curl.

Stir in the reserved liquid and seasoned bread crumbs. Spoon into a baking dish and top with Parmesan cheese. Bake at 350 degrees for 15 to 20 minutes or until bubbly. Serve immediately with melba rounds.

Serves 12

Black Forest Cake

10 tablespoons (1 stick plus 2 tablespoons) butter
1/2 cup sifted all-purpose flour
1/2 cup baking cocoa
6 eggs, at room temperature
1 cup sugar
1 teaspoon vanilla extract
Kirsch Syrup and Cream (page 133)
1 cup drained canned sour red cherries

Melt the butter in a saucepan over low heat. Let stand until the solids settle out of the liquid. Pour off and reserve the clear liquid and discard the solids.

Mix the flour and baking cocoa together. Beat the eggs with the sugar and vanilla in a mixing bowl for 10 minutes or until thickened and nearly tripled in volume. Sift the flour mixture over the egg mixture and fold in gently. Stir in the prepared clarified butter.

Spoon the mixture into 3 generously buttered and floured 7-inch cake pans. Bake at 350 degrees for 10 to 15 minutes or until a wooden pick inserted into the center comes out clean. Cool in the pans for 5 minutes. Loosen the layers from the edges of the pans with a knife and invert onto wire racks.

Pierce the layers with a fork and pour the Kirsch Syrup over the layers. Let stand until cool. Spread each layer with Kirsch Cream and top with the cherries. Stack the layers and garnish the top with chocolate curls and stemmed fresh cherries.

Serves 12

Kirsch Syrup and Cream

KIRSCH SYRUP
3/4 cup sugar
1 cup cold water
1/3 cup kirsch

KIRSCH CREAM
3 cups whipping cream, chilled
1/2 cup confectioners' sugar
1/4 cup kirsch

For the syrup, combine the sugar and water in a saucepan and cook until the sugar dissolves, stirring constantly. Cook for 5 minutes. Cool slightly and stir in the kirsch.

For the cream, beat the whipping cream in a mixing bowl until thickened. Add the confectioners' sugar and beat until soft peaks form. Stir in the kirsch.

Makes enough for 1 cake

Dream Cookies

2 cups all-purpose flour
1/2 teaspoon salt
1 cup (2 sticks) unsalted butter, softened
1 1/4 cups sugar
1 teaspoon crushed baker's ammonium
    (ammonium bicarbonate)
1/2 teaspoon almond extract
1 1/2 cups sweetened flaked coconut

Sift the flour and salt together. Cream the butter and sugar in a mixing bowl until light and fluffy. Beat in the ammonium and almond extract. Add the flour mixture and beat at low speed just until mixed. Mix in the coconut. Shape into a disk and wrap in plastic wrap. Chill for 1 hour or until firm.

Shape the dough into 1-inch balls and place 1 inch apart on a greased cookie sheet. Bake at 300 degrees in the upper third of the oven for 18 to 22 minutes or until light golden brown around the edges. Remove to a wire rack to cool.

Makes 3 dozen

FROZEN BUTTERMILK

Combine one 8-ounce can crushed pineapple with 1 quart buttermilk, 2 cups sugar, one 8-ounce can evaporated milk and 1 teaspoon vanilla in an ice cream freezer container and mix well. Freeze using the manufacturer's instructions.

SAFARI SEND-OFF

*Entering the workforce can be a reason to celebrate!
And since the marketplace is often compared to a jungle,
the safari theme of this party is ideal. After years of
preparation, the graduate is ready for the real world.
With the fun decorating and planning ideas included here—
not to mention the wonderfully exotic menu—you'll be able
to stage the perfect send-off. After such an important
contribution, at least partial claim to your honoree's
future success will be yours!*

CITRUS CREAM TROPICAL KEBABS
SPICY SEARED SCALLOPS
CURRIED ZUCCHINI SOUP
RUM-MARINATED VENISON CHOPS
LIME MOJO RIBS
FESTIVE SHRIMP DIP
GREEN APPLE COCONUT CHUTNEY
THAI SHRIMP SALAD
ARUGULA AND TOMATO SALSA WITH CAPERS
BLACK-EYED PEA SALAD
OKRA AND CORN MELANGE WITH TOMATOES
MANGO TART
WILD ANIMAL COOKIES
TIGER COOKIES

Join us for a
Safari Send-Off
Celebrating
Chad's Graduation

Friday, June 6th
7 P.M.
The Zoo & Botanical Gardens
Stacey & Frank Brown
850-2200

Citrus Cream Tropical Kebabs

CITRUS CREAM
1 cup sour cream
2 tablespoons sugar
2 tablespoons fresh lime juice
1 1/2 tablespoons grated lime zest

KEBABS
1 papaya, peeled and seeded
1/2 pineapple, peeled and cored
3 large bananas
1 tablespoon fresh lemon juice

For the cream, combine the sour cream, sugar, lime juice and lime zest in a small bowl and mix well. Chill, covered, until serving time.

For the kebabs, cut the papaya and pineapple into twenty-four 1-inch pieces. Cut each banana crosswise into 8 slices and combine with the lime juice in a bowl, coating well.

Alternate the fruit on eight 12-inch bamboo skewers. Arrange on a platter and place the Citrus Cream in the center.

You may substitute orange or lemon juice and zest for the lime juice and zest if perferred.

Serves 8

Spicy Seared Scallops

1 (12-inch) daikon
5 romaine leaves, finely shredded
6 tablespoons all-purpose flour
1 tablespoon each ground cumin and coriander
3/4 teaspoon ground cardamom
1 1/2 teaspoons each coarse salt and cayenne pepper
24 sea scallops

Peel the daikon and cut into 1/4-inch slices. Arrange on a serving platter and top each with the shredded lettuce.

Mix the flour, cumin, coriander, cardamom, salt and cayenne pepper in a bowl. Cut the scallops into halves and coat with the flour mixture.

Heat a medium nonstick skillet over medium heat and spray with nonstick olive oil cooking spray. Add the scallops and sear for 1 minute on each side or until golden brown. Place each scallop on a daikon slice. Serve warm or at room temperature.

Daikon is an Asian radish, available in better supermarkets or Asian markets.

Makes 48

Decorate for a safari party with brightly colored African and animal prints, mosquito netting, bamboo, vines, palmettos, binoculars, safari hats, baskets and canvas chairs. Use peanuts instead of oasis for exotic flower arrangements and provide a steel drum band or other African-influenced music. Drinks could be served in plastic canteens with neck straps, which could also double as party favors.

Curried Zucchini Soup

8 small zucchini
3 cups chicken stock
1 cup chopped onion
1 garlic clove, minced
1 teaspoon curry powder
1/2 cup milk
1/2 cup heavy cream
salt and pepper to taste

Cut the zucchini into 1-inch slices. Combine with the chicken stock, onion, garlic and curry powder in a large saucepan and simmer until the zucchini is tender. Process the mixture in a blender until smooth.

Combine the mixture with the milk, cream, salt and pepper in a large bowl and mix well. Chill for several hours.

Ladle into soup bowls and garnish with a dollop of sour cream and parsley sprig.

Serves 6

Rum-Marinated Venison Chops

1 cup apple juice
1/2 cup teriyaki sauce
1/2 cup honey
1/2 cup dark rum
3 garlic cloves, crushed
2 tablespoons minced fresh gingerroot
1 tablespoon dry mustard
1 teaspoon Worcestershire sauce
8 (1-inch) venison chops
1 cup apple jelly
1/4 cup teriyaki sauce
3 tablespoons lime juice
1/8 teaspoon ground nutmeg

Combine the apple juice, 1/2 cup teriyaki sauce, honey, dark rum, garlic, gingerroot, dry mustard and Worcestershire sauce in a shallow dish or sealable plastic bag. Add the venison chops and cover or seal. Marinate for 8 hours or longer, turning occasionally; drain, reserving the marinade.

Combine the reserved marinade with the jelly and 1/4 cup teriyaki sauce in a saucepan and mix well. Bring to a boil and reduce the heat. Simmer for 15 to 20 minutes or until reduced to 1 1/2 cups, stirring occasionally. Stir in the lime juice and nutmeg.

Grill the venison chops for 20 minutes or until done to taste, brushing occasionally with the sauce. Serve with the remaining sauce.

Serves 8

Lime Mojo Ribs

2 tablespoons ground cumin
1/2 cup olive oil
1/4 cup minced seeded jalapeño peppers
6 garlic cloves, minced
1/2 cup chopped fresh cilantro
3/4 cup fresh lime juice
3 tablespoons sherry vinegar
1 teaspoon salt
1 teaspoon pepper
5 pounds pork ribs

Toast the cumin in a heavy skillet over medium heat for 4 minutes or until fragrant, stirring frequently. Heat the olive oil to 175 degrees in a large heavy saucepan. Remove from the heat and stir in the cumin.

Add the jalapeño peppers, garlic, cilantro, lime juice, vinegar, salt and pepper and mix well. Cool completely.

Grill the pork ribs until done to taste. Serve with the lime mojo.

Serves 4 to 6

Green Apple Coconut Chutney

1 teaspoon cumin seeds
3 to 4 Granny Smith apples, peeled and chopped
1 teaspoon (or more) lemon juice
1/2 cup fresh coconut
1/2 bunch cilantro
2 garlic cloves
2 to 3 serrano chiles
3/4 teaspoon salt

Toast the cumin seeds in a small heavy skillet over high heat until a rich brown and fragrant, stirring frequently. Spread on a plate to cool, then process in a food processor.

Toss the apples with the lemon juice and combine with the coconut, cilantro, garlic and serrano chiles in a food processor. Pulse to chop. Add the toasted cumin seeds and salt and process until coarsely chopped. Adjust the lemon juice and salt to taste.

Serve with the grilled pork ribs as an alternate to the lime mojo or with other grilled meats.

Makes 4 to 5 cups

Thai Shrimp Salad

3 cups water
1 pound fresh shrimp
2 tablespoons sliced green onions
1 tablespoon finely chopped lemon grass or
   lemon peel
3/4 tablespoon chopped seeded red chile
1 garlic clove, minced
1 tablespoon lemon juice
1 tablespoon fish sauce
2 teaspoons vegetable oil

Bring the water to a boil in a saucepan and add
the shrimp. Simmer for 2 to 3 minutes or until
the shrimp are pink and opaque. Drain, peel and
devein the shrimp.

Combine the green onions, lemon grass, red chile,
garlic, lemon juice, fish sauce and vegetable oil in a
bowl and mix well. Add the shrimp and toss to
coat well.

Chill, covered, in the refrigerator. Toss again before
serving. Serve on a lettuce-lined plate.

Serves 3 or 4

ARUGULA AND TOMATO SALSA WITH CAPERS

Chop and seed 1 pound of plum tomatoes
and combine with 2/3 cup lightly packed
chopped fresh arugula or basil in a bowl. Add
1 chopped shallot, 1 1/2 tablespoons drained
capers, 1/2 cup olive oil and 2 tablespoons
fresh lemon juice and toss to mix well.

Black-Eyed Pea Salad

1 1/2 cups dried black-eyed peas
3 cups water
salt to taste
1 cucumber, peeled, seeded and chopped
1 small red onion, chopped
1 large tomato, diced
1 serrano chile, seeded and finely chopped
1/2 cup chopped fresh parsley
1/2 cup chopped fresh chives
1 teaspoon salt
1/2 teaspoon freshly ground pepper
juice of 1 lemon
1/3 cup olive oil

Combine the peas with the water and salt to taste
in a saucepan and bring to a boil. Reduce the heat
and simmer, covered, for 15 to 20 minutes or until
tender; drain.

Combine with the cucumber, onion, tomato,
serrano chile, parsley and chives in a bowl and
mix well. Season with 1 teaspoon salt and pepper.
Marinate, covered, for several hours.

Add the lemon juice and olive oil at serving time
and toss to mix well. Adjust the seasonings.

Serves 8

Okra and Corn Melange with Tomatoes

4 slices bacon
1 onion, finely chopped
kernels from 4 ears fresh corn
2 cups sliced okra
3 large tomatoes, peeled and chopped
1 small green bell pepper, chopped
1 teaspoon sugar
Tabasco sauce to taste
salt and pepper to taste

Fry the bacon in a skillet until crisp. Remove and crumble the bacon; drain the skillet, reserving 1/4 cup drippings in the skillet.

Add the onion, corn and okra to the drippings. Sauté for 10 minutes, stirring constantly. Add the tomatoes, bell pepper, sugar, Tabasco sauce, salt and pepper. Simmer, covered, for 25 minutes or until done to taste.

Adjust the seasonings. Spoon into a serving dish and top with the crumbled bacon.

Serves 6

Mango Tart

1 sheet frozen puff pastry, thawed
1 egg, lightly beaten
1 tablespoon sugar
1/2 cup sour cream
1/3 cup whipped cream cheese
3 tablespoons sugar
1 teaspoon lime juice
1 tablespoon finely grated lime zest
2 large mangoes, peeled

Unfold the puff pastry sheet and invert on a greased baking sheet; trim the edges with a sharp knife. Brush to the edge with the egg; do not allow egg to drip over the sides. Score a 1/2-inch border around the edges of the pastry, taking care not to cut all the way through. Prick the inner rectangle with a fork and sprinkle with 1 tablespoon sugar.

Bake at 400 degrees in the lower third of the oven for 15 minutes or until puffed and golden brown. Remove to a wire rack to cool.

Combine the sour cream, cream cheese, 3 tablespoons sugar, lime juice and lime zest in a mixing bowl and whisk until smooth. Spread over the cooled pastry. Cut the mangoes lengthwise into thin slices. Arrange over the cream cheese mixture. Garnish as desired.

Serves 8

Wild Animal Cookies

COOKIES
2 1/2 cups all-purpose flour
1/4 teaspoon salt
1 cup (2 sticks) butter, softened
3/4 cup sugar
1 egg
1 teaspoon orange extract or other extract flavors
1/2 teaspoon grated orange zest, lemon zest or
   cinnamon (optional)

JUNGLE FROSTING
2 egg whites
3 1/2 cups (about) confectioners' sugar
2 teaspoons orange extract
food coloring (optional)

For the cookies, mix the flour and salt together. Cream the butter and sugar in a mixing bowl until light and fluffy. Beat in the egg, orange extract and orange zest. Add the flour mixture and beat at low speed just until mixed. Shape into a disk and wrap in plastic wrap. Chill for 1 hour.

Roll the dough 1/4 inch thick on a lightly floured surface. Cut with wild animal cookie cutters and arrange on a greased cookie sheet.

Bake at 350 degrees for 8 to 10 minutes or until golden brown. Cool on the cookie sheet for 5 minutes; remove to a wire rack to cool completely.

For the frosting, beat the egg whites in a mixing bowl until soft peaks form. Add the confectioners' sugar and orange extract gradually, beating constantly until stiff peaks form. Color as desired with food coloring. Spread or pipe on the cookies.

Makes 3 dozen

Tiger Cookies

2 cups all-purpose flour
1 teaspoon baking soda
1/2 teaspoon salt
3/4 cup (1 1/2 sticks) butter, softened
1 cup sugar
2 eggs
1 teaspoon vanilla extract
3 cups sugar-frosted corn flakes, crushed
1 cup (6 ounces) semisweet chocolate chips

Mix the flour, baking soda and salt together. Cream the butter in a large mixing bowl until light. Add the sugar gradually, beating constantly until fluffy. Beat in the eggs. Stir in the vanilla. Add the flour mixture and mix well. Stir in the cereal.

Melt the chocolate chips in a double boiler over simmering water. Add to the dough and mix just enough to swirl the chocolate through the dough; do not overmix.

Drop by heaping teaspoonfuls 2 inches apart on an ungreased cookie sheet. Bake at 375 degrees for 10 to 12 minutes or until golden brown. Remove to a wire rack to cool.

Makes 5 dozen

Entertaining Casually

Sometimes a not-so-serious gathering is in order. Don't wait until you're too old to wear purple—have a little rambunctious fun now! While two of these ideas are fairly unique, the Cinco de Mayo party can be altered for any celebration. Go ahead, be a little crazy!

GATHERING OF THE GODDESSES

COME AS YOU ARE

CINCO DE MAYO

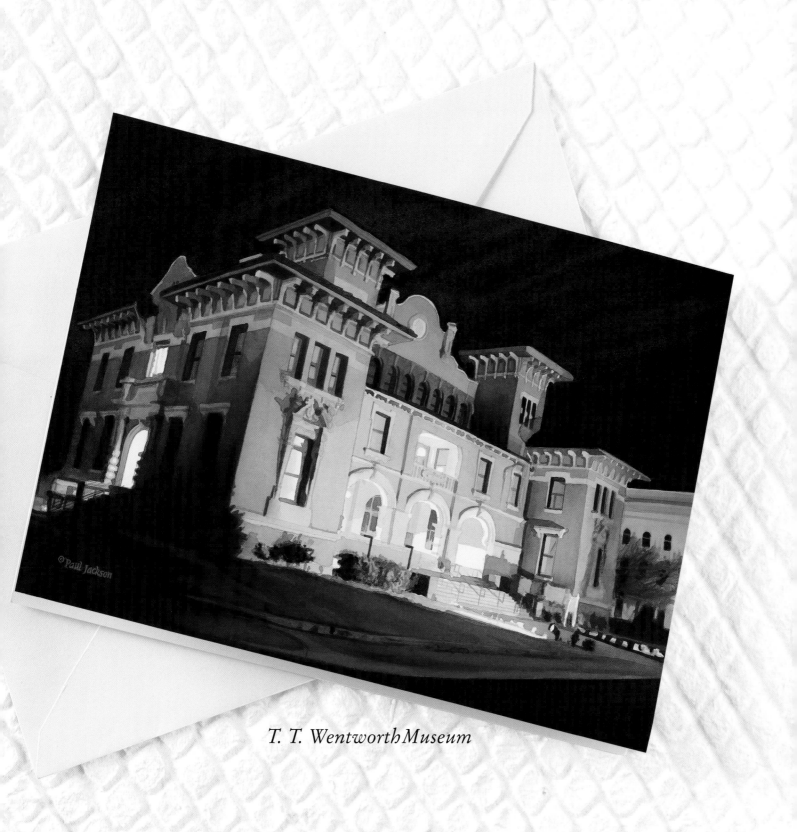

T. T. Wentworth Museum

Gathering of the Goddesses

*Southern women don't just make friends—we make **girlfriends.** Girlfriends understand each other, know each other's secrets and love each other anyway. Perhaps our attachments stem from our attitudes about being women—we're comfortable in our own skins and, frankly, like to keep them moisturized. Want to feel good about being female? Plan a casual evening for your girlfriends—simple menu, comfortable surroundings, and plenty of time to indulge in a pedicure—now **that's** a night to remember!*

Greek Antipasto

Parmesan Twists

Skopelos' Crab Patties

Martha's Vineyard Salad with Raspberry Maple Dressing

Grilled Vegetable Pizza

Chocolate Fondue

GATHERING OF
GODDESSES

A Celebration
of Girlfriends
Join me for a night fit
only for Queens!

Friday, May 4th
6:00 PM
Shannon Cook

Pensacola Spa
850-5555

Greek Antipasto

2 pounds fresh shrimp, cooked and peeled
16 ounces kalamata olives
1 jar pepperoncini
2 (4-ounce) jars marinated artichoke hearts
8 ounces fresh mushrooms
1 1/2 pounds feta cheese, cut into bite-size pieces
1/2 cup olive oil
1/2 cup fresh lemon juice
oregano and garlic salt to taste

Combine the shrimp, olives, pepperoncini, artichoke hearts, mushrooms and cheese in a large sealable container. Toss to mix well and drain.

Combine the olive oil, lemon juice, oregano and garlic salt in a cup and mix well. Add to the shrimp mixture and mix well. Seal the container and marinate in the refrigerator for 6 hours or longer, shaking several times.

Spoon the mixture onto a serving platter and garnish with lemon slices.

You may reserve a portion of the marinade from the artichoke hearts and add it to the olive oil mixture if desired.

Serves 12

Surround the goddesses with every form of hedonistic pleasure at this party. Greet guests at the door with fuzzy slippers, pillows and a crown. Provide someone to give manicures and pedicures. Send them home with favors of fingernail polish, lip gloss, lotion, and chocolates.

Pensacola has long been the home of great women. Mariana Bonifay, a French-born businesswoman who arrived in the area in 1784, is known as Pensacola's first matriarch. She became a driving force in the construction of new homes, pioneering the brick industry and operating brick kilns near the clay bluffs on Escambia Bay.

Parmesan Twists

1/4 cup (1/2 stick) butter or margarine, softened
1 cup (4 ounces) grated Parmesan cheese
1/2 cup sour cream
1 cup all-purpose flour
1/2 teaspoon Italian seasoning
1 egg yolk, lightly beaten
1 tablespoon water
caraway seeds or poppy seeds

Cream the butter in a mixing bowl until light. Add the Parmesan cheese and sour cream gradually, beating constantly until smooth. Mix the flour and Italian seasoning together. Add to the creamed mixture and mix to form a dough.

Divide into 2 portions and roll each portion to a 7×12-inch rectangle on a lightly floured surface. Cut each into 1/2×6-inch strips. Twist each strip 2 or 3 times and place on a greased baking sheet.

Beat the egg yolk with the water in a cup. Brush over the strips and sprinkle with caraway seeds. Bake at 350 degrees for 10 to 12 minutes or until light brown.

Makes 4 1/2 dozen

Skopelos' Crab Patties

6 slices white bread
2 eggs
1/4 cup heavy cream
1 tablespoon lemon juice
1 pound crab meat, flaked
4 green onions, finely chopped
4 slices bacon, crisp-cooked and crumbled
1/2 teaspoon dry mustard
2 teaspoons Cajun spice mix
salt and pepper to taste
2 cups cracker crumbs
vegetable oil

Trim the crusts from the bread and process the bread into crumbs in a food processor. Add the eggs, cream and lemon juice and process until smooth.

Combine the mixture with the crab meat, green onions, crumbled bacon, dry mustard, Cajun spice mix, salt and pepper in a bowl and mix well. Shape into patties. Coat with the cracker crumbs. Sauté in a small amount of vegetable oil in a skillet until golden brown on both sides.

Thanks to Skopelos On The Bay for this recipe.

Serves 4

Martha's Vineyard Salad with Raspberry Maple Dressing

RASPBERRY MAPLE DRESSING
1/2 cup raspberry vinegar
1 cup olive oil
1/2 cup maple syrup
2 tablespoons Dijon mustard
2 tablespoons dried tarragon leaves, or
   1/4 cup chopped fresh tarragon
salt to taste

SALAD
8 cups loosely packed mixed baby salad greens, or
   1 medium head green leaf lettuce, torn
1/2 head red leaf lettuce, torn
1/4 cup (1 ounce) crumbled bleu cheese
12 (1/4-inch) slices red onion, separated into rings
3 tablespoons roasted walnuts or toasted pine nuts

For the dressing, combine the raspberry vinegar, olive oil, maple syrup, Dijon mustard, tarragon and salt in a bowl and mix well.

For the salad, mix the baby salad greens and the lettuce in a large bowl. Add 3/4 of the dressing and toss to coat well. Spoon onto 6 chilled serving plates. Top with the bleu cheese, onion rings and roasted walnuts. Drizzle with the remaining dressing.

You may prepare your own raspberry vinegar by combining 1 cup each white wine vinegar and red wine vinegar with 1/2 cup fresh or frozen raspberries in a jar. Let stand for 48 hours. Strain and store at room temperature.

Serves 6

Grilled Vegetable Pizza

1/2 cup balsamic vinegar
1 cup olive oil
3 garlic cloves, minced
1 tablespoon chopped fresh rosemary
1 tablespoon chopped fresh thyme
2 small zucchini
2 small yellow squash
1 red bell pepper
1 green bell pepper
1 large sweet onion
salt and pepper to taste
4 unbaked pizza crusts made from Pizza Dough
   (at right)
1/2 cup (2 ounces) grated Parmesan cheese
1 1/2 cups (6 ounces) shredded mozzarella cheese
1 1/2 cups (6 ounces) crumbled fresh goat cheese
3 or 4 Roma tomatoes, seeded and chopped
1/2 cup shredded fresh basil leaves

Combine the balsamic vinegar, olive oil, garlic, rosemary and thyme in a medium bowl and mix well. Let stand at room temperature for 15 minutes or in the refrigerator for a longer period. Cut the zucchini and yellow squash into rounds. Cut the onion into thick wedges. Cut the bell peppers lengthwise into strips. Arrange the vegetables on a baking sheet and sprinkle with salt and pepper. Brush with some of the vinegar mixture.

Grill over medium coals for about 8 minutes or until tender-crisp and lightly charred, turning occasionally and basting with the vinegar mixture.

Grill 2 pizza crusts at a time over medium coals for 3 minutes or until the top puffs and the bottom is crisp. Turn and grill for 1 minute longer. Invert onto a work surface.

Sprinkle the pizza crusts with the Parmesan cheese, mozzarella cheese and grilled vegetables. Top with the goat cheese, tomatoes and basil. Drizzle each with 1 1/2 teaspoons of the remaining vinegar mixture.

Place 2 pizzas at a time on the grill with a large metal spatula. Close the grill or cover loosely with foil and grill until the crusts are cooked through and the cheeses melt, rotating occasionally to cook evenly.

For a really easy party, use purchased boboli crusts and grill the vegetables in advance. At party time all you have to do is grill the pizzas. You may add sausage for heartier pizzas or vary the vegetables to suit the season and individual tastés.

Makes 4

Pizza Dough

1 tablespoon sugar
1 envelope dry yeast
1 cup (105- to 115-degree) water
3 tablespoons olive oil
3 cups (or more) all-purpose flour
1 teaspoon salt
1 tablespoon chopped fresh basil

Sprinkle the sugar and then the yeast over the warm water in a food processor. Let stand for 10 minutes. Add the oil and process until smooth. Add 3 cups flour and the salt and process for 1 minute or until the mixture forms a ball.

Remove to a lightly floured surface and sprinkle with the basil. Knead for 5 minutes or until the dough is smooth and elastic, kneading in additional flour if the mixture is sticky. Place in an oiled large bowl and turn to coat the surface. Let stand, covered, for 1 hour or until doubled in bulk.

Punch down the dough and knead for 2 minutes or until smooth. Divide into 4 portions and press each portion to a 9-inch circle on the floured work surface.

Makes 4 crusts

Unsweetened chocolate is hardened pure chocolate liquor also known as bitter or baking chocolate. Chocolate liquor contains about 45 percent solids and 50 percent cocoa butter.

Cocoa is a highly concentrated powder produced by hydraulically pressing finely ground unsweetened chocolate. The process removes most of the cocoa butter, leaving a powder relatively low in fat when compared to chocolate.

Semisweet chocolate is chocolate liquor that contains varying amounts of vanilla, sugar, and emulsifiers. Semisweet chocolate contains a minimum of 35 percent chocolate liquor, although the highest qualities contain much greater amounts.

Chocolate chips must have a fat content of about 30 percent in order to hold their shape during baking. For best results, buy chocolate chips that list cocoa butter as the fat additive rather than palm oil.

White chocolate is essentially milk chocolate without cocoa solids. US law requires that products labeled "chocolate," however, must contain cocoa solids. Read product labels carefully to see if it really is white chocolate, or if it is actually confectionery coating.

Chocolate Fondue

6 (1-ounce) squares unsweetened chocolate
1 1/2 cups sugar
1 cup light cream
1/2 cup (1 stick) butter
1/8 teaspoon salt
1/4 cup crème de cacao

Melt the chocolate in a heavy saucepan over low heat. Add the sugar, cream, butter and salt and mix well. Cook over medium heat for 5 minutes or until thickened, stirring constantly. Stir in the crème de cacao. Spoon into a fondue pot or chafing dish. Serve with mandarin oranges, marshmallows and lace cookies for dipping.

Makes 3 1/2 cups

Chocolate...women...happy times...sad times...they all seem to go together. Chocolate has been offering comfort since it was first brewed by the Indians of Central and South America from the pods of the cacao trees. Montezuma was so convinced of the power of chocolate as an aphrodisiac that he drank 50 cups a day, but his was flavored with chile peppers.

The idea of eating chocolate didn't develop until two hundred years later. We no longer think of it as an aphrodisiac, but it does have qualities that many of us find irresistible, having both the ability to perk us up and to calm us down. There is evidence that it may actually lower cholesterol, but women know that its real appeal is to the soul. It is almost as much comfort as a close girlfriend and the combination is unbeatable.

Come As You Are

Want to join some friends in throwing a party that no one will ever forget? This is it!
Each hostess is commissioned to take a surprise photograph of several guests before the party.
What makes the party memorable is that the guests must "come-as-they-were"
when the pre-party photograph was taken—in pajamas, wedding gown, or wrapped in a towel.
It's easier on the guests than a costume party and twice as entertaining!
A guaranteed hit—we promise!

Fruit Salsa with Cinnamon Crisps

Parsley Pecan Dip for Vegetables

Mushroom Palmiers

Praline-Topped Brie

Chicken Cordon Bleu

Pork on Rosemary Skewers

Dilly Smoked Salmon Spread

Cheesy French Bread

White Chocolate Cranberry Cookies

Toffee Cheesecake Bars

Brownie Dessert Cups

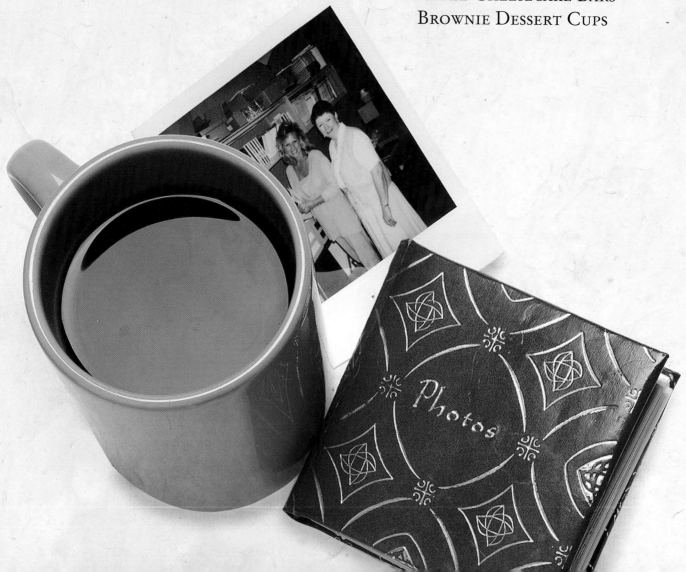

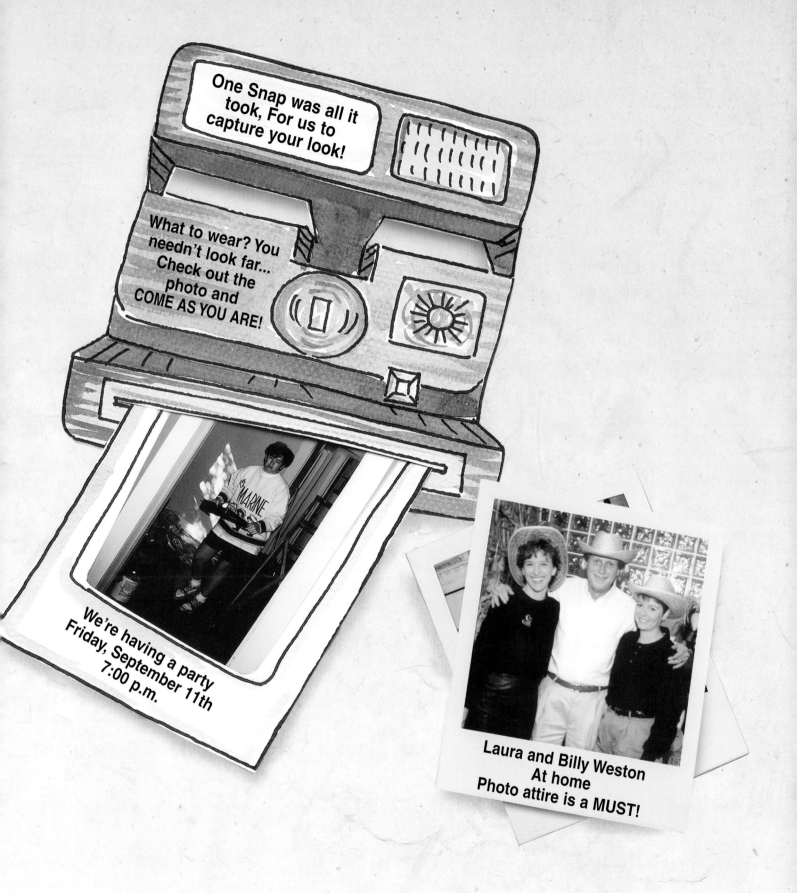

Fruit Salsa with Cinnamon Crisps

CINNAMON CRISPS
1 tablespoon sugar
1/2 teaspoon ground cinnamon
4 (7-inch) flour tortillas

FRUIT SALSA
2 medium Granny Smith apples
juice of 1 small orange
1 kiwifruit, peeled and chopped
1 cup sliced strawberries
grated zest of 1 small orange
2 tablespoons brown sugar
2 tablespoons apple jelly or red plum jelly

For the crisps, mix the sugar and cinnamon in a cup. Spray the tortillas lightly with water and sprinkle with the cinnamon mixture. Cut each tortilla into 8 wedges with a pizza cutter.

Arrange the wedges in a single layer on a baking sheet. Bake at 375 degrees for 4 to 6 minutes or until light brown and crisp. Remove to a wire rack to cool completely.

For the salsa, peel and slice the apples. Combine with a small amount of the orange juice in a food processor and pulse once or twice to chop. Remove to a bowl.

Combine the kiwifruit and strawberries in the food processor and pulse once or twice to chop. Add to the apples and mix well. Stir in the remaining orange juice, orange zest, brown sugar and apple jelly. Serve with the cinnamon crisps.

Serves 16

Enlarge the surprise photographs taken for the invitations to the party to use as table decorations. Ask guests to bring photographs of themselves as children and circulate them to see who can identify the most. Invite a photographer to snap photographs of couples during the party and send guests home with the framed photos as favors.

Parsley Pecan Dip for Vegetables

1 garlic clove
1/2 cup chopped parsley
1/2 teaspoon paprika
salt and cayenne pepper to taste
2 cups sour cream
1/2 cup toasted pecans

Chop the garlic in a food processor. Add the parsley and process until finely chopped. Combine with the paprika, salt and cayenne pepper in a bowl and mix well. Add the sour cream and pecans and mix well. Let stand for several hours to blend the flavors before serving. Serve with vegetables for dipping.

This is also good stuffed in cherry tomatoes or added to cottage cheese and served on a salad of tomato slices and lettuce leaves.

Makes 3 cups

Mushroom Palmiers

5 tablespoons olive oil or butter
16 ounces mixed wild mushrooms or
 button mushrooms, chopped
1 or 2 medium onions, finely chopped
2 garlic cloves, minced
2 tablespoons all-purpose flour
1/4 teaspoon (or less) sugar
Worcestershire sauce to taste
3/4 teaspoon lemon juice
2 teaspoons dried thyme
salt and pepper to taste
2 sheets frozen puff pastry, thawed
1 egg
2 teaspoons water

*H*eat the olive oil in a large skillet over medium heat. Add the mushrooms, onion and garlic and sauté until the vegetables are tender and the liquid has evaporated, stirring occasionally. Stir in the flour, sugar, Worcestershire sauce, lemon juice and thyme. Cook for 2 minutes, stirring constantly. Season with salt and pepper.

Place 1 sheet of the puff pastry on a work surface and spread with half the mushroom mixture. Roll both short sides tightly toward the center to enclose the filling and press the rolled sides together. Place on an ungreased baking sheet. Repeat with the remaining puff pastry and mushroom mixture.

Chill, covered, in the refrigerator for 1 hour or longer until firm. Cut into 1/4-inch slices. Brush with a mixture of the egg and water. Bake at 350 degrees for 20 minutes or until golden brown. Serve warm.

Makes 3 dozen

Praline-Topped Brie

1 (13- to 15-ounce) Brie cheese round
1/2 cup orange marmalade
1 tablespoon bourbon or dark rum
3 tablespoons brown sugar
1/3 cup chopped toasted pecans

*P*lace the Brie in a shallow ovenproof serving dish. Combine the marmalade, bourbon and brown sugar in a small bowl and mix well. Spread over the cheese and sprinkle with the pecans. Bake for 15 to 20 minutes or until the cheese is soft and the topping is bubbly. Serve with crackers.

Serves 8

*P*ensacola's Museum of Commerce is a favorite destination for young and old alike. Housed under the roof is a reconstructed street scene from the 1890s, with hardware, toy, leather and music shops. There is also a collection of antique presses in the print shop and several horse-drawn buggies. The museum can be leased for parties.

Chicken Cordon Bleu

5 medium boneless skinless chicken breasts
5 ounces semisoft cheese with garlic and herbs
2 1/2 ounces very thinly sliced cooked ham
1/2 cup fine dry seasoned bread crumbs
1 tablespoon chopped fresh parsley
1/2 cup milk
1 tablespoon butter or margarine, melted

Place each chicken breast between 2 pieces of plastic wrap and place rib side up on a work surface. Pound 1/4 inch thick with the flat side of a meat mallet, working from the center to the edges. Remove the plastic wrap and spread the chicken with the cheese. Place the ham over the cheese and trim the edges to fit.

Fold in the long sides of the chicken pieces and roll from the short sides to enclose the filling; secure with wooden picks.

Mix the bread crumbs and parsley in a shallow dish. Dip the chicken rolls in the milk and then into the bread crumb mixture, coating well. Arrange seam side down in a rectangular 2-quart baking dish sprayed with nonstick cooking spray. Drizzle with the melted butter.

Bake at 400 degrees for 30 to 35 minutes or until the chicken is cooked through and light brown. Chill in the refrigerator for 2 hours. Cut crosswise into 1/2-inch slices and serve chilled.

Makes 40 slices

Pork on Rosemary Skewers

LEMON ROSEMARY MARINADE
2/3 cup chicken broth
4 teaspoons lemon juice
1/2 teaspoon grated lemon zest
2 teaspoons honey
1 teaspoon chopped fresh rosemary leaves, or
   1/4 teaspoon crushed dried rosemary leaves
1/8 teaspoon salt
1/4 teaspoon pepper

PORK
1 pound boneless lean pork
12 (6-inch) rosemary twigs or bamboo skewers

For the marinade, combine the chicken broth, lemon juice, lemon zest, honey, rosemary, salt and pepper in a small bowl and mix well.

For the pork, soak the rosemary twigs in water to cover in a bowl for 30 minutes or longer. Cut the pork into 3/4-inch cubes. Combine with the marinade in a sealable plastic bag and turn to coat well. Marinate in the refrigerator for 1 to 2 hours.

Drain the pork, reserving the marinade. Drain the rosemary twigs. Thread 4 pieces of pork on each twig and brush with the reserved marinade. Grill, uncovered, over medium coals for 10 minutes or until the pork is cooked through and the juices run clear, turning once.

Serves 4

*E*ither smelt roe or caviar can be used in the Dilly Smoked Salmon Spread. The only difference is that only salted sturgeon roe can be sold as caviar. Others must prefix the name of the fish. Beluga caviar from the beluga sturgeon in the Caspian Sea is considered the best, but it is also the least available and most expensive due to overfishing in the Caspian Sea. The United States is now producing domestic caviar from sturgeon and other species as well, including smelt.

Caviar is made by removing the roe sac from the fish; the eggs are then separated, washed, salted, dried, and packed in cans. Caviar can be stored unopened in the refrigerator for up to 3 weeks; caviar that has been opened should be eaten within a week. Pasteurized caviar can be stored for up to four months before opening.

Caviar should be served in glass, plastic, or wooden containers. Metal containers that easily oxidize, such as silver or pewter, can react with caviar and impart a metallic taste.

If you choose one of the less expensive caviars, add a splash of fresh lemon juice to perk up the flavor. Whether you choose the most expensive or least expensive caviar, you should never use it in cooked dishes, as cooking toughens the texture and ruins the effect. Instead, add it to your recipe as a final garnish.

Dilly Smoked Salmon Spread

1 (4-ounce) fresh salmon fillet
1/2 teaspoon lemon pepper
1 teaspoon dried dill
1/4 teaspoon lemon juice
1 cup ricotta cheese
16 ounces cream cheese, softened
6 ounces smoked salmon, finely chopped
1/4 cup chopped fresh dill
3 tablespoons (or more) fresh lemon juice
salt and pepper to taste
1/4 tablespoon smelt roe or caviar

*P*lace the fresh salmon fillet in a shallow baking dish coated with olive oil. Top with the lemon pepper, dried dill and 1/4 teaspoon lemon juice. Bake, covered with foil, at 350 degrees for 20 minutes or until opaque. Cool and flake into bite-size pieces.

Combine the ricotta cheese, cream cheese and smoked salmon in a food processor or blender and process until smooth. Remove to a bowl and add the baked salmon, fresh dill, 3 tablespoons lemon juice, salt and pepper; mix well. Adjust the lemon juice if needed.

Chill until serving time. Spread with the smelt roe and serve with vegetables or melba toast.

You may also shape this into individual appetizers and top with fresh dill and smelt roe.

Makes 3 cups

Cheesy French Bread

1 baguette
1/4 cup extra-virgin olive oil
1 cup (4 ounces) goat cheese with herbs
1 cup (4 ounces) ricotta cheese
1 cup (4 ounces) shredded mozzarella cheese
1 large garlic clove, minced
white pepper to taste
18 oil-pack sun-dried tomatoes, drained and
    cut into halves

Cut the baguette into 1/4-inch slices and arrange on a baking sheet. Brush the tops with the olive oil. Bake at 350 degrees for 2 minutes or until golden brown.

Combine the goat cheese, ricotta cheese, mozzarella cheese, garlic and white pepper in a bowl and mix well. Mound 1 teaspoon of the cheese mixture on each bread slice. Top with the sun-dried tomatoes and spread a second teaspoon of the cheese over the top.

Bake for 6 to 12 minutes or until the topping is bubbly. Serve warm.

Serves 6 to 8

White Chocolate Cranberry Cookies

1 1/2 cups all-purpose flour
1 teaspoon baking soda
1 cup (2 sticks) butter, softened
3/4 cup sugar
3/4 cup packed brown sugar
1 egg
1 teaspoon vanilla extract
1 1/2 cups rolled oats
1 cup dried cranberries
1 cup (6 ounces) white chocolate chips
1 cup (6 ounces) toffee chips

Sift the flour and baking soda together. Cream the butter, sugar and brown sugar in a mixing bowl until light and fluffy. Beat in the egg and vanilla.

Add the flour mixture gradually, mixing well after each addition. Add the oats, cranberries, white chocolate chips and toffee chips gradually, beating constantly at low speed.

Chill in the refrigerator or place in the freezer until firm. Drop onto a cookie sheet. Bake at 350 degrees until light golden brown. Cool on the cookie sheet for 5 minutes and remove to a wire rack to cool completely.

Makes 5 dozen

Toffee Cheesecake Bars

1 1/4 cups all-purpose flour
1 cup confectioners' sugar
1/2 cup baking cocoa
1/4 teaspoon baking soda
3/4 cup (1 1/2 sticks) butter
8 ounces cream cheese, softened
1 (14-ounce) can sweetened condensed milk
2 eggs
1 teaspoon vanilla extract
1 3/4 cups (10 ounces) toffee bits

Mix the flour, confectioners' sugar, baking cocoa and baking soda in a medium bowl. Cut in the butter until crumbly. Press over the bottom of an ungreased 9×13-inch baking pan. Bake at 350 degrees for 15 minutes.

Beat the cream cheese in a mixing bowl until light. Add the sweetened condensed milk, eggs and vanilla and beat until smooth. Stir in 1 cup of the toffee bits. Spread over the hot crust. Bake for 25 minutes longer. Cool on a wire rack for 15 minutes.

Sprinkle the remaining toffee bits evenly over the top. Cool to room temperature. Chill in the refrigerator before cutting. Store in the refrigerator.

Makes 3 dozen

Brownie Dessert Cups

coarse sugar or decorating sugar
1/2 cup (1 stick) unsalted butter, cut into pieces
5 ounces bittersweet chocolate, coarsely chopped
4 egg yolks
2 tablespoons sugar
2 egg whites
2 tablespoons sugar

Butter the 4 end cups of a 6-cup nonstick jumbo muffin pan and sprinkle lightly with coarse sugar. Combine the butter and chocolate in a double boiler or heatproof bowl and place over simmering water. Heat until the butter and chocolate melt, stirring occasionally.

Combine the egg yolks with 2 tablespoons sugar in a bowl and whisk until the mixture is thick and pale yellow. Fold in the chocolate mixture.

Whisk the egg whites until soft peaks form. Add 2 tablespoons sugar and whisk until stiff and shiny but not dry. Fold into the chocolate mixture. Spoon into the prepared muffin cups.

Bake at 350 degrees for 25 minutes or until set and slightly springy to the touch. Cool in the pan on a wire rack for 15 minutes. Loosen carefully from the muffin cups with a knife and remove to serving plates. Serve with praline ice cream, mocha ice cream, mint chocolate chip ice cream or the ice cream of your choice.

This recipe is most successful if it is not doubled.

Serves 4

CINCO DE MAYO

People from all over the world have settled in the Pensacola area during our long history. The cultural diversity, coupled with a marvelous climate, means that a festival of one variety or another can be found practically every weekend. Cinco de Mayo (Fifth of May) is a celebration of a battle won by a relatively smaller army of Mexicans against the French in 1862. It calls for music, dancing and, of course, authentic Mexican fare. Include all of your amigos in this family-friendly party!

MEXICAN CHEESECAKE WITH SALSA ROJA

SOUTHWESTERN CHEESE SPREAD

PICO DE GALLO

BORDER BUTTERMILK

AVOCADO AND PEACH SALSA

AVOCADO CRAB DIP

HOMEMADE KAHLÚA

CHICKEN RELLENOS

SHRIMP QUESADILLAS

SOUTHWESTERN PASTA SALAD

MARGARITAS

MEXICAN SOUR CREAM CORN BREAD

SWEET LIME BREAD

FIESTA COOKIES

PLATANOS FRITOS

Olé Amigos!

Celebrate Cinco de Mayo
May 5th at 7:00 P.M.

Barkley House Grounds
Caroline Hartnett

Please say
"si si" 432-1234

Sombreros
optional!

Mexican Cheesecake with Salsa Roja

1¹/4 cups crushed tortilla chips
¹/4 cup (¹/2 stick) unsalted butter, melted
16 ounces cream cheese, softened
2 cups (8 ounces) Monterey Jack cheese, shredded
3 large eggs
¹/2 cup sour cream
1 (4-ounce) can chopped green chiles
1 cup picante sauce
¹/2 cup sour cream
1 avocado, mashed
lime juice and picante sauce to taste
garlic powder, salt and pepper to taste
Salsa Roja (at right)

Mix the crushed tortilla chips with the melted butter in a bowl. Press over the bottom of a greased 9- or 10-inch springform pan. Bake at 350 degrees for 10 minutes.

Process the cream cheese and Monterey Jack cheese in a food processor until smooth. Add the eggs and ¹/2 cup sour cream and pulse to mix. Add the green chiles and 1 cup picante sauce and mix well. Spread over the baked crust and place on a baking sheet. Bake for 40 minutes.

Spread ¹/2 cup sour cream over the top. Cool to room temperature on a wire rack. Chill in the refrigerator. Remove the side of the springform pan and place the cheesecake on a serving plate.

Combine the avocado with lime juice, picante sauce, garlic powder, salt and pepper to taste in a bowl and mix well. Spread over the cheesecake. Spread Salsa Roja over the avocado mixture and garnish the center with a dollop of sour cream. Serve with tortilla chips.

Serves 14

It's easy to decorate for a south-of-the-border party. Drape tables with serapes and center them with cacti and bright flowers in colorful pottery. Add wooden serving plates, baskets, sombreros and mariachi music. Hang a piñata from the trees and encourage guests to try their hand at a true Mexican tradition. Adorn a donkey with a bright serape and a sombrero and take pictures of guests to send home with them as favors. Bottles of Homemade Kahlúa (page 162) also make festive favors.

Salsa Roja

3 large tomatoes, chopped
1 red onion, minced
1 garlic clove, minced
2 serrano peppers, minced
1 bunch cilantro, minced
¹/4 cup fresh lime juice

Combine the tomatoes, onion, garlic, peppers and cilantro in a bowl. Add the lime juice and mix well. Chill, covered, in the refrigerator.

Makes 4¹/2 cups

Southwestern Cheese Spread

2 cups (8 ounces) Cheddar cheese, shredded
1 cup (4 ounces) Swiss cheese, shredded
1 cup (4 ounces) Monterey Jack cheese, shredded
2 tablespoons chopped green bell pepper
2 tablespoons chopped yellow bell pepper
2 tablespoons chopped red bell pepper
2 tablespoons chopped green onions
1 1/2 teaspoons capers
3/4 teaspoon minced garlic
3/4 teaspoon Worcestershire sauce
1 1/2 teaspoons chopped fresh dill
3 tablespoons chopped fresh cilantro
Tabasco sauce to taste
3/4 teaspoon Cajun seasoning
2 to 3 tablespoons Dijon mustard
1/4 to 1/2 cup mayonnaise
Pico de Gallo (at right)

Mix the Cheddar cheese, Swiss cheese and Monterey Jack cheese in a large bowl. Add the bell peppers, green onions, capers, garlic, Worcestershire sauce, dill, cilantro, Tabasco sauce and Cajun seasoning and mix well. Stir in the Dijon mustard and mayonnaise.

Line a 1-quart bowl with plastic wrap, leaving a 4-inch overhang. Press the cheese mixture into the bowl and fold the overhang over the top. Cover with additional plastic wrap and chill until serving time.

Unfold the plastic wrap and invert the mold onto a serving plate. Spread with Pico de Gallo and serve with tortilla chips or assorted crackers.

Serves 16

Pico de Gallo

1 cup chopped red tomato
1 cup chopped yellow tomato
1 cup chopped green tomato
1/2 cup finely chopped red onion
2 garlic cloves, minced
1/2 fresh jalapeño pepper, seeded and minced
1/4 cup chopped fresh cilantro
1 tablespoon chopped fresh parsley
1 tablespoon chopped fresh chives
1/3 cup olive oil
1/4 cup red wine vinegar
1 tablespoon fresh lemon juice

Combine the tomatoes, onion, garlic, jalapeño pepper, cilantro, parsley and chives in a large bowl. Add the olive oil, vinegar and lemon juice and mix well. Chill, covered, for 4 hours.

Makes 6 cups

The grounds of the Barkley House make a wonderful setting for a Cinco de Mayo party. The house was built around 1820 by the English trader George Barkley. The architecture represents the only remaining example of a Creole high house in Pensacola.

Avocado and Peach Salsa

1 avocado
1 1/2 fresh peaches
1 large cucumber
1/2 cup chopped red bell pepper
2 green onions, thinly sliced
2 tablespoons chopped cilantro
1 1/2 tablespoons lime juice
1 tablespoon olive oil
1/2 teaspoon crushed dried red chile

Peel the avocado and peaches and cut into 1/2-inch pieces. Peel, seed and chop the cucumber. Combine the avocado, peaches and cucumber with the bell pepper, green onions and cilantro in a bowl. Add the lime juice, olive oil and crushed chile and mix well. Serve with crackers and melba toast.

Serves 8

Avocado Crab Dip

2 large avocados, peeled and chopped
2 tablespoons lemon juice
8 ounces cream cheese, softened
2 tablespoons (1/8-inch) green onion slices
1 teaspoon chopped garlic
1/2 teaspoon Worcestershire sauce
1/4 teaspoon pepper sauce
1 (6-ounce) package crab meat, drained and flaked

Toss the avocados with 1 tablespoon of the lemon juice in a bowl. Combine the remaining 1 tablespoon lemon juice with the cream cheese in a medium bowl and mix well. Stir in the green onions, garlic, Worcestershire sauce and pepper sauce. Fold in the crab meat and avocados gently.

Spoon into an ovenproof dish. Bake at 350 degrees for 15 to 20 minutes or until heated through; stir and serve with crackers, tortilla chips or corn chips. You may also omit the baking and serve cold or at room temperature.

Serves 12

Chicken Rellenos

RELLENOS
4 chicken breasts
2 ounces Muenster cheese
4 canned whole green chiles
1/4 cup bread crumbs
1 1/2 teaspoons grated Parmesan cheese
chili powder to taste
1/8 teaspoon cumin
1/8 teaspoon pepper
3 tablespoons butter, melted

SAUCE OLÉ
1 (8-ounce) can tomato sauce
2 tablespoons chopped green onions with tops
1/4 teaspoon Tabasco sauce
1/4 teaspoon cumin
1/4 teaspoon salt

For the rellenos, pound the chicken to 1/4 inch thickness with a meat mallet on a work surface. Cut the cheese into 4 pieces and place 1 piece in each chile. Place 1 chile on each piece of chicken and roll the chicken to enclose the chile; secure with wooden picks if necessary.

Mix the bread crumbs, Parmesan cheese, chili powder, cumin and pepper in a shallow dish. Roll the chicken in the butter and then in the bread crumb mix, coating well.

Place seam side down in a shallow baking pan. Drizzle any remaining butter over the rolls. Bake at 400 degrees for 30 minutes or until the chicken is cooked through.

For the sauce, combine the tomato sauce, green onions, Tabasco sauce, cumin and salt in a small saucepan. Cook over medium heat for 5 minutes or until heated through. Serve over the chicken rolls.

Serves 4

Shrimp Quesadillas

1/2 cup (2 ounces) small shrimp
1/2 cup chopped tomato
1/2 cup (2 ounces) crumbled feta cheese
1/3 cup chopped fresh dill
1/4 cup chopped green onions
1/4 teaspoon hot pepper sauce
1 cup (4 ounces) shredded mozzarella cheese
4 (8-inch) flour tortillas

Combine the shrimp, tomato, feta cheese, fresh dill, green onions and pepper sauce in a bowl and mix well. Place the tortillas on a work surface and sprinkle 2 tablespoons mozzarella cheese over half of each tortilla. Spoon the shrimp mixture over the cheese and top with the remaining mozzarella cheese. Fold the tortillas over to enclose the filling and press the edges together.

Cook the quesadillas 2 at a time in a heated nonstick skillet over medium heat for 3 to 5 minutes or until light brown on the bottom. Turn the quesadillas and cook until the cheese is melted and the bottom is light brown. Cut into wedges to serve.

Serves 4

Southwestern Pasta Salad

3 ounces cream cheese
1/4 cup lime juice
3 tablespoons milk
1 tablespoons olive oil
1 teaspoon grated lime zest
1 garlic clove, minced
1/2 teaspoon cumin
1/2 teaspoon chili powder
1/4 teaspoon salt
2 tablespoons grated Parmesan cheese
2 cups bow-tie, penne or spiral pasta,
   cooked and drained
1 (16-ounce) can black beans, rinsed and drained
1 1/2 cups cooked corn kernels
1 (4-ounce) can chopped green chiles, drained
1/4 cup chopped tomato
1/4 cup chopped cilantro
1 green onion, chopped
3/4 cup (6 ounces) Cheddar cheese

Combine the cream cheese, lime juice, milk, olive oil, lime zest, garlic, cumin, chili powder and salt in a microwave-safe bowl. Microwave on High for 1 minute or until the cream cheese is softened. Stir to mix well, adding a small amount of warm water if needed for the desired consistency. Stir in the Parmesan cheese.

Combine the cream cheese mixture with the hot drained pasta in a bowl and toss gently to mix well. Add the beans, corn, green chiles, tomato, cilantro, green onion and Cheddar cheese. Toss to mix well.

Serves 6

MARGARITAS

Fill a blender 2/3 full of ice and add one 6-ounce can frozen limeade concentrate. Add 1 juice can tequila, 1/2 juice can Triple Sec, 1 egg white and 1 teaspoon salt. Blend until smooth and serve immediately.

Mexican Sour Cream Corn Bread

1 cup yellow cornmeal
1 tablespoon baking powder
1 1/2 teaspoons salt
chopped onion and jalapeño pepper to taste
1/2 cup vegetable oil
2 eggs
1 cup sour cream
1 (8-ounce) can cream-style corn

Combine the cornmeal, baking powder and salt in a bowl. Add the onion, jalapeño pepper, vegetable oil, eggs, sour cream and corn and mix well.

Coat a heavy baking pan generously with shortening. Heat in a 375-degree oven until very hot. Spoon the batter into the prepared pan and bake at 375 degrees for 30 to 40 minutes or until golden brown.

Serves 4

Sweet Lime Bread

BREAD
3 cups all-purpose flour
2 teaspoons baking powder
1 teaspoon salt
4 eggs, beaten
1 cup milk
1 cup (2 sticks) butter or margarine, softened
2 cups sugar
2 tablespoons grated lime zest

LIME GLAZE
1/2 cup sugar
3 tablespoons fresh lime juice
finely grated lime zest to taste

For the bread, sift the flour, baking powder and salt together. Beat the eggs with the milk in a bowl. Cream the butter, sugar and lime zest in a mixing bowl until light and fluffy. Add the dry ingredients to the creamed mixture alternately with the egg mixture, mixing well after each addition.

Spoon into 2 lightly greased 4×8-inch loaf pans or 5 miniature loaf pans. Bake at 350 degrees for 55 minutes or until golden brown for large loaf pans. Bake miniature loaves for 45 minutes or until loaves test done.

For the glaze, combine the sugar, lime juice and lime zest in a small saucepan and cook over low heat until the sugar dissolves, stirring constantly.

Pierce holes in the tops of the loaves and drizzle the warm glaze over the warm loaves. Cool in the pans until the glaze soaks in. Remove to a wire rack to cool completely.

Makes 2 large or 5 miniature loaves

Fiesta Cookies

12 (6-inch) flour tortillas
1/2 cup (3 ounces) semisweet chocolate chips
3/4 teaspoon shortening
1/4 cup confectioners' sugar, sifted
1/2 teaspoon freshly ground cinnamon

Cut each tortilla into 8 wedges and place on an ungreased cookie sheet. Bake at 400 degrees for 10 to 12 minutes or until light brown.

Combine the chocolate chips and shortening in a microwave-safe bowl or double boiler. Microwave or heat for 1 to 2 minutes or just until melted, stirring frequently. Keep warm.

Combine the confectioners' sugar and cinnamon in a large sealable plastic bag. Add the hot tortilla wedges a few at a time to the confectioners' sugar mixture and shake gently to coat well. Arrange in a single layer on waxed paper. Drizzle with the chocolate. Chill until serving time.

Makes 80

PLATANOS FRITOS

Peel and slice plantains, or cooking bananas, 1 to 2 inches thick. Pound gently with a mallet to flatten. Fry in butter in a skillet until golden brown and sprinkle lightly with salt.

Events Worth Entertaining

Every community hosts events that call for celebrating: festivals and holidays, local shows and competitions or even homecoming at the local high school. Make the occasion more memorable by entertaining your friends and family with one of these great party plans.

THE ANGLER'S TABLE

FEAST DE RÉSISTANCE

BLUE ANGEL AIR SHOW
BEACH PARTY